ROSCOE METHODIST CHURCH, LEEDS:

A UNIQUE HISTORY

Compiled and published by Roscoe Methodist Church

2011

Dedicated to the Glory of God and in service with the community

Published by Roscoe Methodist Church
Francis Street
Leeds LS7 4BY
United Kingdom
www.leedsmethodist.org.uk/roscoe.htm

1st impression October 2011
2nd impression (with minor revisions) October 2011

ISBN: 978-0-957-00490-0

Printed by imprint**Digital**.net
Upton Pyne
Exeter
Devon EX5 5HY
UK

Illustrations:

Front cover: Looking out to Chapeltown Road, Leeds, from the chancel of Roscoe Methodist Church

Back cover: Roscoe Methodist Church congregation June 2011

PREFACE

Stop and think for a few moments about the people and places that have had a significant influence on your life......

This short book is a story of people and one unique place – Roscoe Methodist Church in Chapeltown Leeds – and the influence it has had on community life spanning three centuries from 1862 to the present day. The new church building, opened in 1974, stands on the site of Willow House, where Methodists first met together in Chapeltown, and replaced the Roscoe Place Chapel built in 1862. The Roscoe story is however about far more than just buildings and dates as the memorial opening plaque of the new building records:

'...to the glory of God and for service to all people in the community....'

In an influence stretching far beyond its location and size, Roscoe Church has had an impact on countless individuals and families, on the development of the community in Chapeltown, on political and cultural life in Leeds and it has even had global reach! As the current Minister of Roscoe approaching its 150th anniversary, I can witness to the still vibrant commitment of the people who are Roscoe in worshipping God and serving their community. The pages of this book reveal brief glimpses of the many faithful lives that have gone before them and whose influence can still be felt both locally and globally (the international Wesley Guild movement begun at Roscoe in the late 1800s is just one example). Alongside the 'facts and figures' of Roscoe's history can be found a number of 'reminiscences' that give a deeply personal perspective on the unfolding years. From members of the Vickers family who owned Willow House to the stories of those who arrived from the Caribbean as part of the 'Windrush' generation and found a welcome at Roscoe that enabled them to become the community.

All people of a unique place.

i

Producing a book such as this is no easy undertaking, so whilst much thanks needs to be given to all those who have contributed, particular mention must go to Miss Dorothy Lunn (who instigated the collection of reminiscences), the group who co-ordinated it all (including Mr John Vickers, Mrs Clarita Wenham, Mrs Irene Bottomley, Mrs Mary Saddler, Ms Monica Sanders and Revd Mark Harwood) and especially to Revd Trevor Bates and Mrs Yvonne Herbert who did the majority of the research and collation. Special thanks for photographs go to Leroy Wenham for front cover, to Hughbon Condor for back cover, and to Ken Wenham for that of the church on page 160, and to John Summerwill for his magnificent help with graphic preparations prior to printing. Thanks also for the grant received from the Leeds Philosophical & Literary Society towards production costs.

As you read and reflect on the people and places recorded here, give thanks to God for those who have influenced your life.

Revd Mark Harwood

June 2011

INTRODUCTION

Sometime in the late 1970's my minister at Chapel Allerton Methodist Church (the Revd Stainer Smith) "volunteered" me to go to Roscoe Place Methodist Church to help Sheila Chapman, the wife of the Revd Michael Chapman, at the Sunday School, then on a Sunday afternoon. We entertained anyone over about 12 who came, and brushed the finger print dust off the chairs in a room at the back of the "old" church building before starting. As Stainer pointed out, I could play the piano and had a car. Actually, I usually used a guitar as this meant I could face the teenagers, mainly girls, and get them to sing more and gossip less.

The move to the new church building was a great improvement, especially for the children meeting in the church, as the old one had become decrepit and was cavernous and dark.

My other abiding memory is the Christmas parties. Our department held theirs at the end of January and included the teachers from the younger ones. Some years were extremely cold and I never park in Francis Street without picturing two friends, packed into my Mini with all the props for the games we'd played, peering through the iced-over car windows, while I walked one of the girls home a few streets away as her father had not come to collect her. What amused me most, as I walked back to the car alone, was that Sister Margaret (Horn) had asked how the girl had broken her large front tooth to be told, "I was fighting!"

Others remember a game of Pelmanism which I foolishly started rather late and couldn't persuade the players to stop for the epilogue so they could go home at a reasonable hour.

I only helped at Roscoe Methodist Church for about ten years and it has been a great privilege to be an observer of this book's creation. The history of the church and community has involved so many dedicated people and the book will bring back powerful memories for contributors and readers alike.

I hope it will inspire all who read in their progress through life to see that any contribution, however small, has a part in the whole which is individual and important.

Monica Sanders

CONTENTS

Chapter One
ORIGINS
1862 - 1911

A Roscoe Methodist Church has been a landmark on Chapeltown Road, Leeds since the second half of the 19th century. We also believe that the people who belong to Roscoe have been an influential force for good in the Chapeltown community across the years.

BEGINNINGS

Wesleyan Methodism in Leeds started in William Shent's barber's shop in Briggate, next door but one to the "Kings Arms". Due to the powerful preaching of John Nelson, a Birstall stonemason, there was a huge crowd ready to listen to Charles Wesley (brother of John Wesley, the founder of Methodism) when he preached from the doorway of the barber's shop on May 29th 1743. By this time there already existed a small Methodist congregation of about fifty people.

The first Methodist Chapel in Leeds was built in 1751 around Matthew Chippendale's house. When finished, the house was pulled down from inside and removed. This "Old Boggart House Chapel" survived until 1849, and **Mr Benjamin Randall Vickers** (1798-1881) was a Class Leader there until he went to Brunswick Chapel. Today this land is swallowed up by the West Yorkshire Playhouse on the site of the former Quarry Hill flats. Brunswick Chapel, the mother chapel of Leeds East circuit, was opened off Wade Lane in 1825. By 1851 Leeds had 13 Wesleyan, 6 Wesleyan Methodist Association, 5 Methodist New Connexion and 6 Primitive Methodist chapels. This clearly indicates that the internal conflicts which resulted from dissensions in Wesleyan Methodism were reflected in Leeds. It was the outreach work into the Little London area, initiated by folk from the Brunswick congregation, which helped to pioneer the way so successfully for the Roscoe Place congregation to be formed.

Brunswick Wesleyan Chapel, Leeds—mother church of outreach work to Little London (1846) and Roscoe Place Wesleyan Chapel (1862)

Methodism came into Chapeltown as a result of other events in the life of the city of Leeds in the 19th century. "Already there were a few houses about the top of Buslingthorpe Lane, two or three on the east side of Chapeltown Road, and a few in Francis Street, Spencer Place and Cowper Street. But the land from the Barracks to Cowper Street was laid out for building, and the houses were rapidly rising there." *('Notes & History of Roscoe', Benjamin Threlfall Vickers)* "In 1828 a housing development known as New Leeds was planned at Squire's

Pasture, part of the Earl Cowper estate north of Barrack Road. This was the start of present day Chapeltown. It was bounded by Leopold Street, Cowper Street, Spencer Place and the Leeds-Harrogate Turnpike Road. The plots were intended for merchant families and the houses were larger than usual with more facilities."(*'A History of Modern Leeds', Frazer, p.101)*

In 1849 a great cholera epidemic ravaged Leeds as well as other towns. Benjamin Randall Vickers, who lived in St. Mary's Square, though not personally affected, decided to move his family to a greenfield site further away from the town centre and bought a plot on Chapeltown Road at the corner of Francis Street in an area where four or five streets were being laid out. There Benjamin, a local preacher and class leader, built **Willow House** in 1852 and included in it a preaching room which served as a meeting place for Methodists in that new area so far removed from any other Methodist chapel.

Willow House, built at the corner of Chapeltown Road and Francis Street, in 1852, which contained the Methodists' preaching room

The **Preaching Room** services were held every Sunday afternoon, conducted by Town Missionaries, and every Thursday evening, conducted alternately by the ministers of the Brunswick circuit and by the Town Missionaries. (The last Town Missionary to minister there died at the ripe old age of 95.) Among the ministers who preached there were the Revds Alfred Barrett, Thomas Vasey, George Maunder, Edward Lightfoot, G. W. Oliver MA, W. B. Pope and John Rattenbury (member of a family well known in Leeds Methodism for several generations). A Mr Benjamin Wood brought the remnant of his Society Class to Willow House after unhappy days in the Wesleyan Reform movement. When Roscoe Place Chapel was built the Preaching Room was closed. The bible, the preaching desk, the forms (benches) and the Class (fellowship) were taken to Roscoe Place. **Benjamin Threlfall Vickers (BTV)** said, "It might almost be said that my father's Preaching Room was the first Roscoe Chapel."

LITTLE LONDON SUNDAY SCHOOL

This commenced in 1846 and was held in a small building behind Victoria Place, Camp Road which was crowded "to suffocation". Benjamin Threlfall Vickers and his father-in-law, **Mr William Farrar Smith,** with **Mr H. H. Legg** attempted, in about 1856, to raise funds for a new school but failed. By 1860 the need for a new school was urgent. Mr Farrar Smith invited the ministers and leading laymen in the Circuit to a tea on October 12th at his own house – Hope Villa in Woodhouse Lane. Mr William Smith, in whose house, Allerton Hall, Gledhow, the Missionary Breakfast Meetings had been held for many years, refused to enter any scheme which did not include a large reduction of the debt on Brunswick Chapel (around £6000). He had himself gifted the organ for Brunswick Chapel.

A meeting was held in the Vestry under the Brunswick Chapel on October 19th 1860 to launch a scheme. 'It was my good fortune, although only a youth, to get into the meeting, 'wrote Benjamin Threlfall Vickers (who listed those who attended). By the end of the meeting subscriptions reached £2402. BTV writes:

"I now have the original Resolution setting out the Scheme:

1. To build a new Little London Sunday School,
   free of debt - £700
2. To build a New Chapel at Sheepscar,
   to seat 1,000 people   free of debt - £3-4000
3. To reduce the debt on Brunswick Chapel - £2000

I have a vivid remembrance of the enthusiasm which pervaded the whole Circuit with this Extension Scheme, which I heartily shared; indeed I am indebted to the Scheme for my first introduction to working Wesleyan enthusiasm."

The architects selected were Messrs Pritchett and Son from Darlington. (James Pigott, Pritchett Jnr's grandfather, was a Congregationalist minister). Little London **Sunday School** was opened on March 16th 1862 and the land for the **Roscoe Chapel site** was purchased for 2s 6d *(two shillings and six old pence)* per square yard. The Little London Sunday School continued to be very active and significant until 1934.

ROSCOE: THE FOUNDATION STONE AND OPENING

A Contract for Work agreement was drawn up on May 8th 1861 between:
    Joe Lindley of Leeds in the County of York, plumber and glazier, and George Smith of Leeds, Woollen Merchant,
    for erecting a Wesleyan Methodist Chapel, Vestries, Chapel Keeper's residence and apartments. Also fencing, drainage and paving. The Chapel to be called Roscoe Place Chapel.

The Foundation Stone was laid by Mr William Farrar Smith and the Revd G.W. Oliver, secretary for the scheme, on Whit Monday, 1861. The Chapel was opened on Friday June 13th 1862. The **Revd Thomas Jackson** (former President of Conference) preached in the morning and the **Revd James Dixon, DD** at night. On the first Sunday, the morning service was conducted by the **Revd Alfred Barrett**. The Opening Services were continued in both Roscoe and Brunswick Chapels for two Sundays and when everything was completed it was found that Roscoe Place began its life with a debt of £2200!

In 1896 electric light was introduced in the Chapel. An organ was borrowed for a time until the first organ was erected in 1864. In 1906 a new organ was about to be installed. It had 31 sounding stops and 1907 pipes with 12 couplers. **Miss Mary Chapman** writes in the May 1972 issue of 'News and Views' (*the Roscoe Place Monthly Newsletter*):

> "It was built to the specification of Mr Norman Strafford, the Roscoe organist at that time. He was a celebrated musician who made a great reputation, not only as a brilliant organist but by his work as a Chorus Master of the Leeds Philharmonic Society and the Leeds Triennial Festival of Music. ...Another (Roscoe Place Chapel) organist, Mr Walter Hartley, became organist at Selby Abbey, a post he held for 40 years."

BTV concludes, 'What of the future? The answer rests with us and those who will succeed us, and partly on the faithfulness of the ministers whom God may send to us. But there is a promise: "As I was with Moses, so I will be with thee. I will not fail thee, nor forsake thee. Be strong and of a good courage" (*Joshua 1:5)*'.

BTV spoke warmly of his father, Benjamin Randall Vickers, who was also a local preacher and class leader. Benjamin Randall Vickers had 'a sound common sense and when required a good strong will'. He had been present in October 1813 when the Wesleyan Methodist Society was established. BTV described his mother (**Margaret Threlfall**) as a lady who was 'gentle, retiring and transparently sincere who devoted herself to caring for the Little London families'. At first there was no Sunday School at Roscoe Place Chapel, Little London being the school for this Chapel. However, in 1882, Roscoe Place School was built at a cost of about £1800 and was enlarged by the addition of the Young Men's Room in 1892.

*(The **Revd William Threlfall** 'the Missionary Martyr of Namaqualand', who was betrayed by his guides and murdered near Warmbaths as he pushed northwards in South Africa in 1826, was Margaret Threlfall's elder brother.)*

6

ITEMS PRESENTED TO THE ROSCOE PLACE CHAPEL

'The Sacramental Service' – Mr Joshua Burton of　　Roundhay

The Communion Table and Cloths – **Mrs Margaret　Vickers** (wife of BRV)

The Font – Mrs J. Smith Weare, Mrs Boddy , Mrs E. M. Jones and Mrs Lobley.

The Gothic Chair – Joseph Hammond LL.B. of Chapeltown, and at that time a local preacher in the Brunswick Circuit.

The Bible and Hymn Book – Mr W. Lomas Joy.

The Pulpit cushion – Mrs Evan M. Jones.'

'The first organ was borrowed. **The first organist** was Mr G. Sidney Smith, grandson of William Smith of Gledhow. The **organ erected in 1864** was by Mr Francis Booth of Wakefield, who was considered one of the best organ builders in England. It had 29 sounding stops, and cost (exclusive of the case and hydraulic engine) £460.'

It is also worthy of note that Roscoe Place Chapel was the first Methodist church in Leeds to have **a spire**.

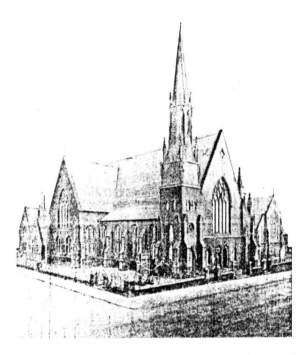

Roscoe Place Wesleyan Methodist Chapel 1914 (notice the spire)

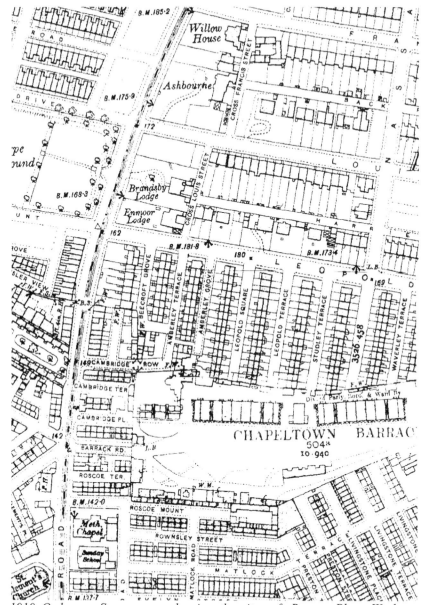

1910 Ordnance Survey map showing the sites of: Roscoe Place Wesleyan Chapel, Sheepscar, and the present-day Roscoe Methodist Church at the junction of Chapeltown Road and Francis Street (built where Willow House stands at the top of this map). Reproduced with permission.

9

SOME MEMBERS OF STAFF

'**Revd James Sugden** who came to the circuit in 1862 had pastoral charge of Roscoe Place. He lived on Louis Street.

First **treasurer of the Trust** – Mr George Smith

First **Secretary** – Mr W. Farrar Smith, who retained office until his death in 1891.

First **Chapel Stewards** – Benjamin Randall Vickers, John Stocks and Morris Simpson.

First **Chapel Keeper** – John Willcock

First **Trustees** – The existing trustees of Brunswick Chapel.

Revd John Rattenbury was **Superintendent** –1867-1869

Another minister was Revd George E. Young – 1870.

A remarkable *female leader, Miss Bowes,* used to meet her Class in her own house on Edmund Street.

Benjamin Threlfall Vickers (*son of Randall and Margaret Vickers*) was **Class Leader** in 1867.'

SIGNIFICANT VENTURES

During this period of 1862 – 1918 there were at least two other significant ventures undertaken by Roscoe Place people. The first was initiated by the **Revd W. Blackburn Fitzgerald** during his ministry 1893 – 1895. This was the pioneering of the **Wesley Guild movement** in 1894, designed to try and attract and hold young people in the life of the Church. The second, which would seem to complement the Wesley Guild venture, was the start of the **13th Leeds Boys' Brigade Company** to hold on to boys and young men, especially from the Little London area where the Sunday School work was so successful. This BB Company was initiated by a group of laymen led by **Mr William Farrar Vickers,** son of BTV.

WESLEY GUILD

Prior to being the minister for Roscoe Place the Revd W. Blackburn Fitzgerald, whilst stationed in the Bolton circuit (*1889-91*) had been working on the idea of establishing a society which would, in his own words, 'co-ordinate all aspects of young people's life'. He introduced the idea to his congregation at his Edgworth chapel, but received no encouragement, and he left the matter until he moved to Roscoe Place and here he found a more receptive people.

In 1894 the Revd Charles H. Kelly, Book Steward and past President of the Wesleyan Methodist Conference, prepared and presented a paper at the London Wesleyan Methodist Council. It was entitled: *How to retain our young people*. He emphasized his concern over the annual loss of young people from the Church. He mentions the existence of the Boys' Brigade, The Band of Hope, the Christian Endeavour Societies and the fact that there were nearly a million scholars in the Sunday Schools, but felt there was still need for another venture.

That same year Charles Kelly was visiting Leeds to speak at a Missionary Anniversary. He met the Revd W.B. Fitzgerald and they compared notes, and found they were both concerned about the same thing – the youth of Methodism.

In 1894 W.B. Fitzgerald had already introduced the subject at Roscoe Place under the heading of **"Guild of the good life"** which was received with favour. His scheme expressed his concerns: about prayer, bible reading, evangelism, overseas mission and for the Guild to have a Look-out Committee. At the Liverpool Wesleyan Methodist Conference in 1896 a whole day was given to the debate which finally inaugurated the Wesley Guild, making it a Connexional organisation answerable to the Conference. Within 10 years of that 1896 Conference launch there were 1920 branches of the Guild with 133,000 members throughout the UK.

Regrettably we have not been able to obtain any historical information of how long the Wesley Guild continued and lasted in the life of Roscoe Place Wesleyan Chapel. Suffice to say that what the Revd W. B. Fitzgerald started at Roscoe caused that venture to be recognised as the beginning of the Wesley Guild movement.

Whilst there may not have been a Wesley Guild at Roscoe for many years, nevertheless the movement is still found throughout the Methodist Church, both in the UK and in other countries. In 1999 the

Wesley Guild movement in the life of the Methodist Church in Ghana celebrated its centenary at Cape Coast. Representatives from the Wesley Guild in the UK, including a former minister of Roscoe, the **Revd Trevor S. Bates,** were invited as guests for that memorable week-long occasion. at which there were about 1,000 delegates from all parts of Ghana.

The most outstanding undertaking by the **Wesley Guilds** in the UK has been the renewed support given to a number of Health Projects (some old and some new) in remote areas of Nigeria and for which £1 million will have been raised by 2010 since the venture started in 1992 for this desperately needed, extraordinary and continuing work.

13TH LEEDS BOYS' BRIGADE COMPANY

It is important to understand the formation of the 13th Leeds Boys' Brigade Company against the background of the events and circumstances of the end of the 19th and the beginning of the 20th centuries in the UK as they pertained to the Wesleyan Methodist Church.

The Boys' Brigade was started in Glasgow in 1883 by William A. Smith, but it was not until 1892 that the Boys' Brigade first appeared in the Leeds area. The formation of the 13th Leeds Boys' Brigade Company connected with Roscoe Place Wesleyan Methodist Church arose out of a real concern for youngsters in the Little London and Sheepscar areas of Leeds. Already there were Sunday Schools in Little London and at Roscoe Place Wesleyan Methodist Church in Sheepscar. Indeed the construction of the Roscoe Place Sunday School building in 1882 was a direct expression of a desire to meet the growing needs of midweek activities for young people sponsored by Roscoe Place Wesleyan Chapel. Whilst the Leeds Battalion and Boys' Brigade Headquarters records indicate that the 13th Leeds Coy was registered in 1909, there is pictorial evidence to show that the first sessions were held in the year 1908/1909. The first Captain was **Mr William Farrar Vickers,** son of BRV.

13TH LEEDS BB COMPANY EVENTS AND ACTIVITIES

1903 – 1908

"The Leeds Battalion was re-constituted and formally enrolled in October 1906….Prior to this – from 1903 to 1906 – Mr W. Farrar Vickers had been acting as Secretary to the Leeds Companies. He resigned, owing to pressure of business, in May 1906. Those who were privileged to work with him at that time testify to the fact that it was due in no small measure to his efforts that once again the B.B. in Leeds could go ahead on a Battalion footing." (p.15 in *"Sure and Stedfast" The History of the Boys' Brigade in Leeds from 1982 to 1942")*

1908 -1920:

Wm Farrar Vickers was the Captain of the 13th during this period and the first Chaplain was the **Revd Walter F. Mayer**.

> "The famous 13th Company is mentioned for the first time (*although not yet by number*) in November 1909 when Mr Vickers informed the (Battalion) Executive Meeting that 'a Company was in course of formation at Roscoe Place Wesleyan Chapel' – this Company was enrolled there on December 8th 1909, after a short period at Little London School, with Mr Vickers as Captain, Revd Walter F. Mayer as Chaplain, and Messrs. **A Allison Armstrong** and **J. Stanley Fearnside** as Lieutenants. Great things were to follow from this Company over the next 30 years. They had been for many years the strongest company in the Battalion and had a most imposing list of honours and achievements". (*p.18/1 in "The History")*

The earliest information of the composition of the 13th BB Coy comes from a photograph taken in 1913 (five years after starting). This shows a company strength of 24 boys with five officers and evidence of a drum (1 base and 2 side drums) and bugle band. The Captain was William Farrar Vickers, and it indicates that the Company was well established by the outset of WWI (*World War One*).

There is no indication that the Company ceased to function at the beginning of WWI. However, whilst "The Great War had little effect on the Boys' Brigade in Leeds at first, and new companies were still being enrolled....As the war progressed and the call for volunteers for the forces, followed by conscription, took away the officers, more and more companies had to cease to meet so that by October 1916 it seems that only the 2nd Coy (Fulneck), 8th Coy (Burley). 11th Coy (Silver Royd Hill), and the 12th Coy (Pudsey) were meeting and even the 2nd Coy had to suspend activities in 1917, but restarted in 1918."*(p.6: "75th Anniversary Brochure BB in Leeds")*

This is confirmed by the report: "The Company was in Camp at Filey in August 1914 when the war broke out, and a number of officers left camp to join up at once. After a short time, owing to there being no available officers, the activities of the Company were suspended until it restarted in 1919 at the urgent demand of the boys in the district..." *(13th BB 21st Birthday Brochure 5th – 8th December 1930).* This brochure also reports that "more than 500 boys have passed out from the Company since its formation 21 years ago, and they are now, we believe, maintaining the high traditions of the Company in every part of the Empire". Photographs of the 13th from that period show the Drum and Bugle Band and a group of boys and officers with a field-cannon on four wheels in the grounds of Roscoe Place Wesleyan Chapel! However, these are undated. In respect of William Farrar Vickers' involvement we note: 'Before and after his marriage to **Doris Simpson**, Farrar participated in the work of the Boys' Brigade in Leeds for much of the time with John Simpson, the brother of Doris.'

"John (Simpson) and I had the wave-lengths of those twelve to eighteen year old lads. Very good use was made of discipline, and there was the most imaginative handling of the boys. In those days we and the other BB officers were as well known as the police in some areas of Leeds. We had to choose the time to go visiting. Sunday dinner was at three or four in the afternoon, and if we arrived at the wrong moment they weren't at all pleased to see us." *(pp 25/6 in 'Spin a Good Yarn')*

No. 10.

WESLEYAN METHODIST
LOAN
TRACT SOCIETY.

LEEDS FIRST CIRCUIT,
1863.

DIVINE WORSHIP

In the following Wesleyan Chapels, viz:— Brunswick Chapel, Roscoe Place, Woodhouse, Chapeltown, Roundhay, Meanwoodside, Thorner and Barwick. Services on the Sabbath, and on one or more evenings in the week.

WESLEYAN SABBATH SCHOOLS,

Brunswick Rooms, Little London, and Lincoln Fields, Leeds.— Woodhouse, Chapeltown, Meanwoodside, Thorner, and Barwick.

WESLEYAN WEEK-DAY SCHOOLS,
DARLEY STREET, LEEDS.

The attention of yourself and family to the above announcements is affectionately requested.

Please read this Tract and keep it Clean,
it will be called for next Sabbath, and another left in its place.

J. Corbridge, Printer, Newsome's Yard, 130, Briggate, Leeds.

Leeds First Circuit Tract No 10, 1863

15

No. 6

ROSCOE PLACE
WESLEYAN TRACT SOCIETY,
1887.

ROSCOE PLACE CHAPEL:—
  Divine Service—SUNDAY at 10.30 a.m. and 6.30
    p.m. MONDAY EVENING at 7.30.
  Baptism—Second Monday in each month. Notice
    to be given to the Chapel-Keeper.
  Prayer Meetings—Sunday Morning at 7, every
    Friday Evening at 7.
  Mothers' Meetings every Monday at 2.30.
  Institute & Literary Society every Friday at 8.
  Sabbath School open at 9.15 a.m., and 2.15 p.m.
  Society Classes every Tuesday, Wednesday and
    Thursday Evenings, and Sunday Afternoons.

LITTLE LONDON SUNDAY SCHOOL:—
  Divine Service every Sunday Evening at 6.30.
  Prayer Meetings—Sunday Morning at 7.
  Band Meetings every Saturday Evening at 7.
  Mothers' Meeting every Tuesday at 2.30 p.m.
  Sabbath School open at 9 a.m. and 2 p.m.
  Young Men's Mutual Improvement Class,
    Friday at 8 p.m.
  Class Meetings every Monday, Tuesday, Wednesday
    and Thursday.

MISSION ROOM, Enfield Rd., Roundhay Rd.
  Divine Service Sunday at 10.30 a.m. and 6.30 p.m.
  Prayer Meetings—Sunday Morning at 7.
  Mothers' Meetings every Monday at 2.30 p.m.
  Sabbath School open at 9.15 a.m. and at 2.15 p.m.
  Class Meetings—Tuesday and Thursday, at 8 p.m.

N.B.—You are affectionately and earnestly invited to
attend any of the above services. Seats provided for all
who come. If any of your family should be afflicted, and
desire the visit of a minister, please inform the distributor
who leaves this tract.

RICHARD CROSLAND, PRINTER, 69, WOODHOUSE LANE, LEEDS.

Roscoe Place Wesleyan Tract No 6, 1887

16

A MATURE CHURCH

On the 1871 Leeds Brunswick Circuit Preachers' Plan Roscoe Place is listed second in the circuit after Brunswick Chapel, and the minister with pastoral charge for Roscoe was also listed second in seniority of the Circuit staff, due to his years of travel, and thus his seniority. We also note that the **Revd John Baker**, minister for Roscoe Place from 1913, died on 12th May 1915. John Baker at the same time was both Superintendent of the Leeds Brunswick circuit and Chairman of the Leeds District. The Roscoe Place Leaders Meeting minutes for June 16th 1915 record a fine tribute to him with a standing vote. John Baker was succeeded by the **Revd W.R. Griffin** as minister for Roscoe.

So by the end of WW1 we get the impression that Roscoe Place Wesleyan Chapel had grown substantially and was capable of moving into the post-war years with vision and energy. Work among children and young people was vigorously supported by a regular pattern of fellowship groups for women and men. A pipe-organ and large choir were also at the heart of the music life of Roscoe.

PLACES & HOURS.		JUNE				JULY		
		4	11	18	25	2	9	16
	HOURS							
BRUNSWICKCHAPEL	10½	Harvard B	Young SS	Willey L	Lord Q	Harvard B	Young H	Willey
	6	Harvard S	Harvard SS	Young	Willey Q	Lord S	Harvard H	Young
							S A	
Wednesday	7	Harvard	Young	Willey	Lord	Harvard	Young	Willey
Saturday Bands	7	Harvard	Young	Young	Lord	Harvard	Young	Flitch
Darley Street Day School		Harvard	Young	Willey	Lord	Harvard	Young	Willey
ROSCOE PLACE... ...	10½	Harvard G. C. †	Harvard	Young	Willey Q	Lord	Harvard H	Young
	6	Harvard G. C. †	Young	Willey	Lord Q	Harvard S	Young H	Willey
Monday	7	Lord	Harvard	Young	Willey	Lord	Harvard	Young
Friday, Prayer Meeting	8	Harvard	Harvard	Harvard	Harvard	Harvard	Harvard	Harvard
Little London Day School		Harvard	Harvard	Harvard	Lord	Harvard	Harvard	Harvard
WOODHOUSE	10½	Willey	Student Q	Harvard	Wilkinson	Willey C	Lord	Harvard H
	2½	Holland	Lofthouse	Johnson	Wilkinson	Clarke	Hammond	Holford
	6	Lomas	Student Q	Lord	Harvard S	Young C	Flitch	Harvard H
Tuesday	7	Lord	Harvard	Young	Willey	Lord	Harvard	Young
Day School...			Willey		Willey		Willey	
CHAPELTOWN	10½	Student	Student	Lord Q	Harvard	Young	Dunning H	Lord
	6	Willey S	Student	Harvard Q	M. Atkinson	Willey S	Lord H	Banks
Thursday	7	Young	Willey	Lord	Harvard	Young	Willey	Willey
Friday, Prayer Meeting	8		Willey		Willey		Willey	
Day School...			Willey		Willey		Willey	
ROUNDHAY	10½	Jones	Lord	Student Q	Young	Armstrong	Willey H	Jackson
	6	Rose	Banks	Student Q	Holland	Shaw	Roadhouse H	Lord S
Thursday	7	Lord		Young		Willey		Harvard
BARWICK	10	Student		Jones	Marsden	Roadhouse		Rose L
	2	Student	Lord MA	Jones	Young Q	Roadhouse	Willey S	Rose
Wednesday...	7		M A	Young		Willey		Harvard
THORNER	10½	Student	Shaw	Lawson	Wilson Q	Heighington	M. Atkinson	Hammond
	6	Student	Holford	Lawson	Young Q	Heighington	Willey S	Hammond
Wednesday...	7			Harvard		Lord		Young
Day School..				Harvard		Lord		Young
BARNBOW	10					Holland		
SCHOLES	6				Marsden	Holland		
WOODHOUSE CARR	10½	Armstrong	Heighington	Jackson	Rose Q	Lawson	Marsden	Wilson T
	6	Student	Student	Student L	Student Q	Learoyd	Wilkinson	Johnson T
Thursday	7	Student	Student	Student	Lofthouse	Shaw	M. Atkinson	Thompson
LINCOLN FIELDS	10½	Young	Clarke	Student	Hammond Q	Holford	Lofthouse H	Armstrong
	6	Wilson	Learoyd	Flitch	Banks Q	Thompson	Fawney H	Heighington
Tuesday	7	Thompson	Rose	Clarke	Holland	Young	Lord	Wilson
Lessons for the Day.	Morn.	Gen. 1	Joshua 10	Judges 4	1 Sam. 2	1 Sam. 12	1 Sam. 15	2 Sam. 12
		Matt. 3	Acts 14	Luke 2	Luke 8	Luke 14	Luke 21	John 4

Part of the Leeds Brunswick Circuit **Plan of the Preachers' Appointments to the Wesleyan Chapels**, *from June 4th to September 24th, 1871. The symbol next to the preachers appointed to Roscoe Place on June 4th is explained as 'Re-opening of Roscoe Place Chapel'. It is not known why or for how long it had been closed so soon after it had been built.*

18

UST		SEPTEMBER				NAMES AND RESIDENCES.
20	27	3	10	17	24	
Lord Willey	Harvard DS Lord DS	Hellier B Harvard S	Willey Young	Lord Q Willey Q	Harvard L Lord	J. H. LORD... ... Brunswick C. H.
Lord Lord Lord	Harvard Harvard Harvard	Young Young Young	Willey Lord Willey	Lord Wilson Lord	Harvard Harvard Harvard	S. P. HARVARD 6, Louis Street G. E. YOUNG ... 9, Blenheim Square W. WILLEY ... ... Chapeltown J. ROADHOUSE .. St. Michael Square
Willey Lord	Baby DS Harvard DS	Harvard Lord S	Young Willey	Willey Q Lord Q	Lord Harvard SA	J. FARRAR President of the Conference J. LOMAS ... ... Headingley
Willey Harvard Lord	Lord Harvard Harvard	Harvard Harvard Harvard	Young Harvard Harvard	Willey Harvard Young	Lord Harvard Harvard	H. H. CHETTLE... Woodhouse Grove B. HELLIER ... Headingley J. PEARSON ... Harrogate
Harvard M. Atkinson M. Atkinson	Willey Q Wilson Young Q	Lord Lawson Lawson	Learoyd Learoyd Chettle S	Pearson MA Thompson Pearson MA	Willey Flitch Student	G. G. FINDLAY, B.A., Headingley J. M. Rany, LL.D. Woodhouse Grove STUDENT ... ... Headingley
Willey Willey	Lord	Harvard Willey	Young	Willey Willey	Lord	B. R. VICKERS... ... New Leeds J. BANKS ... ... Elmwood Green ATKINSON... ... Thorner
Roadhouse Shaw	Young Willey	Young MA Young MA	Harvard Harvard S	Jones Student	Young Q Willey Q	J. W. ROADHOUSE ... Louis Street J. ROSE ... ... Meanwood Terrace
Harvard Willey Willey	Young	Willey Willey Willey	Lord	Harvard Willey Willey	Young	GREEN ... ... 17, Grafton Street W. H. HOLROYD ... 14, Lyddon Terrace E. JONES ... Francis Street, New Leeds
Young Clarke	Johnson Thompson Willey	Willey Flitch	Marsden Wilkinson Harvard	Harvard Q Student Q	Holland Young S Lord	R. THOMPSON... J. J. FLITCH ... Crimbles House J. WILKINSON ... 21, Crawford Street A. LEAROYD 9, Midland Road, Hyde Park
Powney Young T	Jackson Jackson Willey	Willey	Student Student Harvard	Lawson Harvard Q	Wilkinson Wilkinson Lord	W. HOLLAND ... 35, Sackville Street J. MARSDEN ... Francis Street J. LAWSON, 2, Elmwood Grove, Camp Road R. LOFTHOUSE... ... 18, Woodhouse St. J. H. HOLFORD ... 69, Briggate
Holford T Young T	Rose L Rose Lord Lord	Flitch Willey	Student Student Young Young	Roadhouse Q Harvard Q	Johnson Johnson Willey Willey	B. JOHNSON ... ... Woodhouse J. WILSON ... 30, Grafton Street J. DUNNING ... Chapeltown J. CLARKE... ... 87, Queen's Place S. SHAW ... ... Samuel Street
Powney		Hart Hart		Lawson		HAMMOND ... ... Briggate M. ATKINSON. ... Woodhouse Lane J. H. ARMSTRONG ... 93, Briggate J. HEIGHINGTON ...66, Cobourg Street
Rose Harvard S	Banks Hammond	Shaw Student	Lord Student	Holford Q Student Q	Thompson Student	On Trial.
Young	Harvard	Student	Student	Student	Student	G. F. JACKSON J. C. HART J. POWNEY
Holland Jackson	Lord Marsden	Roadhouse Banks L	Student Lord S	Hart Q M Atkinson Q	Learoyd Student	*Any brother who is unable to fulfil his own appointment, shall kindly provide an accredited substitute.
Marsden	Roadhouse	Heighington	Powney	Thompson	Willey	
						Sunday School} Second Monday in every Committee. month, at 8 p.m.
2 Kings 5 Acts 18	2 Kings 10 Acts 26	2 Kings 19 Matt. 4	Jer. 5 Matt. 11	Jer. 35 Matt. 18	Ezek. 2 Matt. 25	Monthly Meeting} First Wednesday in of the Prayer every Month, at 8 p.m. Leaders.

The list of preachers on the same Plan.

19

REMINISCENCES ONE

THE VICKERS FAMILY CONNECTION

BENJAMIN RANDALL VICKERS, born in 1798, was a local preacher as well as a Class leader in the "old Boggart House" in October 1813 when the Wesleyan Methodist Missionary Society was established. In his early life, he had much perplexity as to whether God did not call him to go out as a missionary, but Providence led him to decide otherwise, and he never doubted the correctness of this decision. The business he founded in 1828 (now called Benjamin R Vickers & Sons. Ltd.) is in its 183rd year today with exports worldwide.

Wesleyan Methodism in the New Leeds District dates back to 1852 when he built a Preaching Room in connection with his Willow House, which was then being erected. At that time there was no Place of Worship, and there were only a few houses on Roscoe Place. Until Roscoe Place Chapel was built, it was preceded by the Little London Sunday School built in 1846 – a small building off Camp Road which was crowded to suffocation. When the Chapel was opened, the Preaching Room was closed.

Benjamin Randall married Margaret Threlfall of Hollowforth, Preston in October 1836. She had an elder brother, the Revd William Threlfall, who was one of the first sent by the Wesleyan Methodist Missionary Society to South Africa. When he pushed north, his guides betrayed and murdered him. Margaret named her son Benjamin Threlfall for him.

She went about doing good, bringing an atmosphere of tenderness and sympathy wherever she went. Their family lived and grew up in Willow House at the corner of Francis Street and Chapeltown Road.

Foundations of the Original "Willow House"

In 1849 a cholera epidemic swept through the City of Leeds, and Benjamin Randall Vickers decided to move his family from St Mary's Square out of harm's way further from the city centre. In 1851 he started to build a house in the countryside at Chapeltown, Leeds, where he lived until his death in 1881.

The elder son of BRV was named Benjamin Threlfall Vickers: he married Anne Elizabeth Farrar Smith. Her father, William Farrar Smith, was a JP and a close colleague of the Vickers family in Methodism. Anne Elizabeth devoted great energy in caring for the families located in the little London area. Their own son, named William Farrar Vickers, wrote in 1906 "Alongside Willow House where I lived from 1882 till my marriage to Doris Simpson in 1911, my grandfather built a laundry. Above this was a room where Methodist services were held until eventually Roscoe Place Chapel was built". From that small room developed the Brunswick Methodist Circuit in Leeds. "At the Willow House service of dedication a prayer was said, that on that site there might always be a place of worship to the glory of God, and the service of people".

And so to this day it has been – a Methodist Chapel still stands on the site – "Roscoe Methodist Church".

Besides the outreach to the Leeds community around Little London, some of the Vickers family went far around the world. Farrar's sister Agnes (married to an Irish Methodist minister the Revd Will Vickery) went to Burma; her sister Helen, married to Dr George Hadden, also of Ireland, was a doctor in China. Farrar's brother Randall who married Mabel Gurney, doctored in China, till their return to a practice in Luton and becoming a Vice Chairman of Vickers Oils.

William Farrar Vickers (1882-1977)

21

Likewise Farrar's wife, Doris, was the eldest of seven children of John James Simpson, a pram manufacturer in Hunslet but living in St.Mary's Road, Chapeltown. They were stalwart participants in the life of Roscoe and the family also showed the outreach of that church; the youngest sister was a missionary of Changsha, China for forty years. In those days she stayed in China for six solid years, before one year's home leave.

John Farrar Vickers
(Great grandson of Benjamin Randall Vickers)

MEMORIES OF ROSCOE PLACE

MY HAPPIEST MEMORIES of Roscoe Place are Sundays from 1954 to 1958. Why, because those were the times when life centred entirely round the church. A whole gang of young people around my age spent almost the whole day at church. These people included, but not exclusively, **Joyce Cooper, June Rawnsley, Doreen Barron, Kay Hislop, Malcolm Collett, Peter Thornes**, and my future wife, **Colleen Morgan**.

The day started with Sunday Morning Service, either Boys' Brigade Bible Class in the church hall, (which I will come back to later), once a month was Parade Sunday, when all the uniformed organisations attended morning service in the chapel.

A special Sunday would be if the Boys' Brigade, Leeds Battalion held its annual parade at Roscoe. Some 4 or 500 officers and boys would fill the church to overflowing, even the gallery was full, a truly amazing sight. However, back to Bible Class, **Tom Boyle** usually conducted these classes; they comprised of hymns, accompanied on the piano by **Ernest Poulter**, prayers and the address. Tom did not preach to us, he spoke about life in general, tried in his own way to help us understand there was more to life than back-to-back houses and cobbled streets. I'm not sure I fully understood at the time, but later on this all made sense.

Home for lunch, then back for Sunday school at 2.30, teachers I especially remember were, **Miss Bell, Miss March and Joyce Reyner**, amongst others.

22

After Sunday School a gang of us would stay in the church hall and talk, eat sandwiches which had been prepared by the gang, then later go for a walk for half an hour just before Evening Service.

The day wasn't finished yet. After evening service, it was Sunday Nighters. We all met in a classroom, and sang hymns or perhaps a slide show from Frank Farrar. **Tom Fell and his daughter, Elsie**, would give a musical item. Elsie had an outstanding voice, and I believe she went on to become a professional classic soloist.

Then finally home about 11.00. The end of a wonderful day at Roscoe.

So that is a small memory of Sundays at Roscoe Place Chapel, thank you for allowing me to share it with you.

Brian Ladley

MEMORIES OF JACK LADLEY

1943. MY FIRST MEMORY was as a young boy of just 9. I enrolled in the Life Boys, which was run by a Mr Bee on a Tuesday (?) evening in the schoolroom from 6.30 to 7.30pm; at the same time I was encouraged to join the Sunday School. The Superintendent was Frank Farrar and we had Annual Summer outings to Mr Robert Barr's house in Shadwell. I later (1945) transferred to the Boys' Brigade and our monthly church parades included a Sunday service where the Company officers read the Testament readings and NCOs assisted with the collections.

Early ministers I remember were Revd Blackburn and later Revd Lewis Allison who appeared quite old to us lads but surprised us by joining in a game of soccer at our annual Camp – we later learned he couldn't walk for the rest of the week! I remember Autumn fayres in the Church Hall, stalls selling all manner of produce – followed by an evening talent concert when I played in a very nervous cornet duet. About 1949/50 I also joined the Youth Club and we managed an occasional game of billiards on a magnificent snooker table in the Institute room adjacent to the Caretaker's rooms. I remember Mr Green the caretaker who miraculously appeared every time us lads got up to a bit of mischievousness.

About this time as a Senior boy/NCO we were encouraged to attend Sunday evening church services by our officers Frank Farrar, Ernest Poulter, Harry Cocksedge – who attended regularly with their wives and also an added incentive were the girls who attended from the Youth Club. I remember Elsie Fell who sang wonderful solos – her parents had a fish shop in Roundhay Road. In summer a group of us would occasionally meet after service and were entertained to a cuppa at the manse by Doreen – the minister's daughter (*now Doreen Warmen: see Appendices*). Mr Farnill was a very accomplished church organist.

In 1952 I had to leave Roscoe for a couple of years to satisfy National Service and I had a crash Membership Class before I departed. After National Service I returned as an active officer in the B.B.Company and with a new minister in Harry Salmon who officiated at our marriage on December 24th 1955. We formed new friendships with other officers and wives: Stan and Joan Woodhead, Frank and Elsie Farrar, Tom and Edna Boyle, Harry and Phyllis Cocksedge and Ernest and Olga Poulter.

I continued my association with Roscoe until about 1964/5 when because of my living in Pudsey on the other side of Leeds and working Sunday mornings and with a young family – I had to transfer my membership to Pudsey.

By this time our friends from the Caribbean had started arriving with their carefree happy carnival gay culture and their very welcome influx of vigorous church membership.

Jack Ladley

A SPECIAL WEDDING AT ROSCOE PLACE

AT 2.00 PM ON A WARM AND SUNNY FIFTH OF SEPTEMBER 1959, Roscoe Place Methodist Church held its first ever double wedding, when Sylvia and Patricia Leeming were joined in Holy Matrimony respectively with Harold Bowden and Brian Rudduck.

All four were Church members. Sylvia and Harold taught Sunday-school and Brian was a member of The Boys' Brigade.

The Revd Russell Moston officiated and the church was full with normal congregation and family and friends of both families.

At the organ was Mr Farnill who played the Brides up the aisle – one on each arm of their father – to Walford Davies "Solemn Melody". Two hymns – "Jesus stand among us" and "Love Divine" accompanied the couples vow-taking and a homily by Revd Moston.

After the necessary formalities of signing the Register and to a stirring rendition of the Bridal March, both happy couples walked out into the sunshine.

Sadly Patricia lost her husband Brian when he passed away in 2005. Harold and Sylvia celebrated their Golden Wedding in September 2009.

Sylvia Bowden (formerly Leeming)

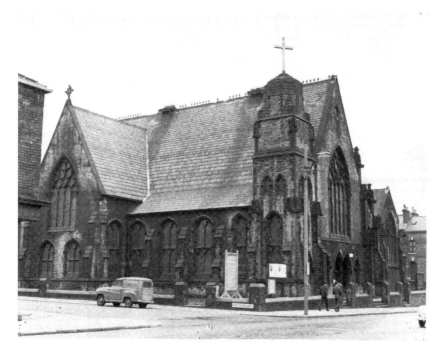

Roscoe Place Wesleyan Chapel. The spire was removed in the 1950s.

Chapter Two
"SURE and STEDFAST"
1911 – 1946

The population of Leeds doubled in size during the first 50 years of the life of Roscoe Place Wesleyan Chapel. In 1862 the population was approximately 250,000 but had grown to around half a million by 1911. We are not surprised therefore that Roscoe Place Chapel found itself being aware of the expanding community of Chapeltown. There was a growing call for strong and wise leadership, vision and enterprise, with a readiness to respond to some of the needs of the homes and families in this expanding community. This was in addition to the work already being maintained in Little London, thus requiring greater sacrificial giving of time, talent, ability, and money.

THE CHANGING CHARACTER OF CHAPELTOWN

Certain indicators of the steady growth and development of the northern area of Leeds, including Chapeltown, need to be mentioned. First, the Jewish community made ventures for greater cohesion and unity among themselves "by opening up negotiations between the four main synagogues of Belgrave Street, New Briggate, Old Central and Byron Street. However, progress did not come easily, yet the beginning of the 20th Century found the 15,000 Jews of Leeds moving in a new direction along North Street and Camp Road, towards Chapeltown and Roundhay, and a new future". *(Louis Saipe in "Leeds Tercentenary Celebrations of the Resettlement of the Jews in the British Isles")*

During this half-century the principal synagogues moved from the centre of Leeds, building afresh in the Chapeltown area, so by the outbreak of WWII there were several new synagogues in this community. The Jewish Moser Memorial Hospital was also built on Leopold Street in 1905 and remained active until its work was handed over to the State in 1946. The Jubilee Hall was built by the Jewish community on Savile Mount in 1936 but needed an extension to be added some years later to cope with the many activities taking place there. These are significant factors in the changing character of Chapeltown.

Secondly, in 1891 an electric tram service was started between Roundhay and Sheepscar, and up Chapeltown Road to Moortown. By the early twentieth century Corporation tramcars were running from 4.30am to 12.30 late night, a clear indication of a growing working population on the move. (*NB evidence of tramcar activity was revealed in May 2010 when road works uncovered tramcar lines in the middle of Chapeltown Road by Cowper Street.*)

Thirdly, 'in 1819 Parliament financed the building of a permanent barracks in Leeds on Barrack Road, Chapeltown, due to social unrest arising from the extreme poverty, unemployment and the aftermath of the Napoleonic wars.' Those barracks were occupied and used by various units of the British Army across the years including the Royal Field Artillery and the Leeds Rifles Battalion, which used the old Riding School and Parade Ground for 80 years until transferred to Harewood Barracks in 1967. The Barracks were eventually demolished in 1988.

ROSCOE PLACE SOLDIERS CLUB

An item in the Trustees Minute Book dated 27th January 1919 indicates that "a statement was read out regarding the Roscoe Place Soldiers' Club giving details of the excellent work being done. A letter of thanks was to be sent to Miss Smith and Mrs Edwin Firth and those associated with them from the beginning. It was resolved that the Soldiers' Club be kept open as long as required and the matter (*of its continuation*) was left to the Committee appointed 29th October 1914." Clearly there was a positive link between Roscoe Place Chapel and the military garrison stationed at the barracks on Barrack Road. Mr Roland Lunn in his memoirs says that Roscoe Place in 1914 was known as "the Garrison Church". Presumably this would be for all those servicemen at the Garrison who were not Church of England (*i.e. Free Church Protestants*).

A **Yorkshire Evening Post** article: (*"Bottled up news finally leaks out, 114 years after being entombed"*) dated December 5th 1975 says "the Roscoe Place Methodist Chapel …accommodated 1,000 worshippers, augmented by men of the 8th Hussars, 17th Lancers and the Royal Artillery from the nearby barracks."

27

ADDITIONAL STAFF FOR LITTLE LONDON

A Wesleyan Deaconess, **Sister Charis**, was working among the people of Little London, which indicates how important that work was. That Wesleyan Mission work had been pioneered by folk from the Brunswick Chapel. The Sunday School work started in 1846, one year after the opening of Brunswick Chapel itself, and a Class Meeting was also started for some of the Members who lived in the neighbourhood.

If the Little London community was marked by the poor living conditions of the people, the stationing of a Deaconess indicates that special attention was being given to this outreach work by the Brunswick circuit and staff. Sister Charis, working there, is mentioned in the Roscoe Place Leaders' Meeting Minutes during the period of 1915/17. However, she became ill and was not able to continue her work beyond September 1917. No mention is made in the Leaders' Meeting Minutes of other Deaconesses for the inter-war years; however, the Roscoe Place Leaders' Meeting of January 1917 states that the Little London Mission work was now placed under their control.

Little London Sunday School was held in the Wesleyan Methodist School building at the corner of Alfred Cross Street and Pattie Street. The Committee Minute Book reports that at the January 1931 meeting **Pastor N. Thomas** was in the Chair with 16 present. This seems to indicate a sizeable Sunday School at Little London, which now came under the care of Roscoe Place. However, at the November 1934 meeting the **Revd C.W. Hickman** was in the Chair and indicated that the School was to be closed after being in existence for 85 years. The children were asked to choose which other Sunday Schools they would like to be transferred to. "Those transferred to Roscoe would be very welcome". At the December 1934 meeting the Sunday School children's parents chose as follows:

> "42 to Roscoe, 20 to Clowes, 18 to Sheepscar Congregational;
> 3 to Cavendish Rd Presbyterian;
> 2 to Meanwood Methodist;
> 1 to St Columba;
> 1 to Eldon;

28

1 to Four Square Tabernacle;
Teachers to accompany the children to Roscoe, Clowes and
Sheepscar Congregational."

A complete listing of the teachers and children is recorded in their groups.

WORLD WAR I WAR MEMORIAL

A special Committee was appointed by the Trustees' Meeting of 13th January 1920 to discuss the possibility of installing a War Memorial in Roscoe Place Chapel listing those who served and those who died in the war. The Committee was very comprehensive: 13 resident Trustees, Poor Stewards, Society Stewards; with one representative from the Sunday School, two from the Choir, one from the Young Men's Institute and the Leaders' Meeting with others.

A year later the Trustees' Meeting of 18th January 1921 was informed of the Committee's recommendation to install a brass tablet in Church which would contain 71 names of men belonging to Roscoe Chapel families: 59 who served and returned, and an additional brass tablet for 12 who served and were killed during World War I. An amount of £71.7s 0d had been contributed to meet the expense involved. (*See Appendix for lists of men*)

GROWING MID-WEEK GROUPS AND ACTIVITIES

We dare to believe that the Roscoe Place congregation was able to hold together people who needed to be helped and people who were in a position to help others. We are not surprised therefore that work among children and young people took high priority among the other standard weekly Chapel activities.

Whilst the **13th Boys' Brigade Company** at Roscoe needed to cease activities in 1916 due to the impact of WWI, in September 1920 the Leaders' Meeting was informed that Mr W. Farrar Vickers and **Mr John Simpson** were proposing to re-start the Boys' Brigade Company, and the Meeting "heard this with pleasure". It was at this re-start that **Harry Cocksedge** became a life boy and remained in the Company

29

until 1942 when he was called to Army service. Harry was Captain for five years (1937-42) and returned to the company after his Army service. On the 31st January 1922 the Leaders' Meeting was informed that W. Farrar Vickers was to hand over the Captaincy to John Simpson at a time when there were 46 boys on roll, with 25 boys in reserve, and an average attendance at Drill and Bible Class of 97%.

The BB Company continued to grow and attract boys and young men, offering them a sense of pride, self-discipline and the opportunity for spiritual growth. The January 1924 Leaders' Meeting was informed that the 13th BB Company had 7 officers, 75 boys and 30 reserves with 95% attendance at Bible Class and 80% for Drill! By the time of its 21st Birthday celebrations in December 1930 the 13th BB Company was one of the most outstanding companies in the Leeds Battalion with a band of at least 18 boys, 3 NCOs (non-commissioned officers) and 2 officers. Bugles, cornets and trumpets with side-drums and a bass drum and a mace bearer are all in evidence in photographs from that era. We are not surprised that apart from the church parades, introduced in Autumn 1927 for the Boys' Brigade and Girl Guides, the BB Bible Class became an acceptable alternative to Chapel worship on Sundays!

It was in the 1920s that the **Harold and Edith Boyle family** came to reside at Roscoe Place Chapel House from Scarborough. Harold was employed as caretaker to the Chapel as from 20th February 1923. Three of the sons were to play a significant part in the life of the 13th Leeds Boys' Brigade Company and of the Chapel. They were Alfred (*known as Jim*), Leonard, and Harold (*known as Tom*). All three became officers and Tom Boyle was Captain for eleven years (1946-54; 1959-62) In 1939 Leonard Boyle became one of the Church Stewards. The Leaders' Meeting Minutes are not clear whether Leonard Boyle was Society Treasurer in 1942, but at the Annual Society Meeting of 21st February 1943 Leonard Boyle presented the balance sheet, so it appears that he was part of the 'finance team'. Regrettably Harold Sr. died of tuberculosis on 20th March 1927, so the family had to vacate the Chapel House and went to live at 42 Cowper Street but retained their involvement with Roscoe Place Chapel.

In spite of the difficult economic times in the country after WW1 (*World War One*) Roscoe Place church life appears to have been robust in the inter-war years. The Leaders' Meeting Minutes indicate that the January 1926 meeting (*when 34 members were present*) received reports from the following groups :

> Sunday School (Mr Reyner & Miss Firth)
> Mothers' Meeting (Miss Fitton)
> Chapel Choir (Mr Haiste)
> Young Leaguers (Miss Walker)
> Girls' League (Miss Fitton)
> Wesley Guild (Mr McCutcheon)
> Young Men's Institute (Mr McCutcheon)
> Boys'Brigade (Mr Bellhouse)
> Sunshine Band (Miss Holmes & Miss Fitton)
> Young Men's Society Class (Mr Frank Farrar)

In the 1930s additional groups and organisations were started: Brotherhood and Sisterhood meetings; a Men's Fireside Group; a Regnal League; a Youth Circle and a Band of Hope with a Temperance Book. A **Girl Guide Company** was also started with Miss Joyce Reyner as Captain. The starting date cannot be established, but was probably in 1927 according to a Leaders' Meeting Minute for September that year. However, a **Brownie Pack** was formed on 17th December 1929. The first Brown Owl was Miss Eileen Gaunt (later a Deaconess) and Miss Dorothy Ramsden was involved with its leadership from 1943 to 1971 when the Pack was closed.

A surprising development is indicated by a letter from the **Roscoe Place Sunday School Council** to the Trustees' Meeting 12th November 1923, urging serious consideration be given to providing additional space to meet the growth of the Primary Department. Decision and action seem to have been delayed until the Meeting of 30th January 1925 when it was decided that the wall between the two vestries in the Chapel building be demolished to make one larger room and so accommodate the need.

It is important not to lose sight of the music side of Roscoe Place Chapel's life. The **Chapel Choir** played an important part in the week to week worship services. The Choir was ably led by Mr **Thomas H. Standeven** until his death in 1932. Thomas Standeven owned a retail

Draper's shop in Frankland Terrace, Chapeltown. At the Trustees' Annual General Meeting of January 1933 the Minutes "record with thanksgiving the long and efficient service of the late Thomas Henry Standeven who was secretary of the Trust. His regular and unobtrusive work was in keeping with the rest of his life which was noteworthy for the amount of voluntary work done in many directions."

Mr Leslie Farnill was appointed **organist** in August 1925 at a salary of £25 per annum with four weeks' notice either side. Leslie was further confirmed as organist and choirmaster by the Trustees' Meeting of 1933. A **Junior Choir** was formed. They gave a concert on 16th March 1940 and a report on their behalf was given at the Leaders' Meeting of August 1941 by Mrs Bilton, their leader. The **13th Boys' Brigade Company Band** was also a unique feature of Roscoe's life, being recognised as the most outstanding BB Band in Leeds.

CONGREGATION SIZE AND FINANCIAL ABILITY

After half a century of activity Roscoe Place Wesleyan Chapel, along with other churches of that time, must have been getting large congregations. The very fact that the Chapel had a gallery indicates the expectations of those whose vision it was to build at Sheepscar. The Leaders' Meeting Minute Book for 1915 reports a membership of 217 with 9 "On Trial". Among the new members listed are Mr Benjamin Threlfall Vickers (son of Benjamin Randall Vickers) and Mrs Vickers (who presumably transferred their membership from the Brunswick Chapel) as well as Mrs Elsie Firth and Mr & Mrs Reyner – all of whom became key people in the life of Roscoe. The same Minute Book in an entry for January 1916 records the appointment of 6 door stewards and 4 gallery stewards – obviously catering for sizeable congregations at Sunday services. We have not been able to find any records of size of congregations for the WWI years and following.

We presume there was still much poverty in the community (especially the Little London area), and wages were basic for those who were working. In the same Minutes for January 1916 an entry reports Mr Haiste (*the Society Treasurer*) indicating that the Society Funds were deficient by £26. 9s 1d on 31st December 1915, and he appealed for an increase in the weekly collections stating, "If we can maintain an average collection of £4. 12s 0d per week, we should without difficulty meet our assessment." Some members took exception to this and there was a long discussion – the main point being that Roscoe Place was too highly assessed. In conclusion it was resolved that no alteration in Circuit Assessment was necessary. If we reason that the average person would be putting 1d or 2d in the collection – and maybe some people nothing, whilst others a ½d; and if the better off members might give 6d or even 1/- then the total congregation on a Sunday at Roscoe Place may well have been several hundred! There being 1104 pence to equal £4.12. 0d! So, could we judge that the average congregations for Sunday Services may well have been 4–500? This would be in line with the 'rule of thumb' practice in Methodism at that time of attendance being about double the membership.

In addition the fact that grants allocated at Christmas 1915 for distribution to the poor were - 10/- each to Mrs Robinson, Mrs Thornbury and Mr T. C. Brown; 5s 0d each to six other leaders/visitors; and 2s 6d to 3 others. In addition £1 to Sister Charis for use among the Poor of Little London; all money to come from the Poor Fund – a total of £4. 7s 6d, almost equivalent to the average weekly collection Mr Haiste (*Society Treasurer*) requested to meet the Circuit Assessment! This seems to indicate at least two conclusions – first, there were a large number of "poor people" connected with Roscoe Place Chapel; and secondly the Poor Fund would seem to accumulate the equivalent of one week's collection across the year for distribution to the needy! This appears to be a very generous distribution.

However, the Roscoe Place Trustees' Minute Book entry for 13th January 1920 reports that the Society Stewards were asking for assistance from the Trustees in meeting an increased assessment. A special grant of £25 was given "for this year only. The Trustees and Leaders to look into the whole question of Finance". The Trustees Minutes' report, at the December 1921 meeting, that the Envelope System of giving was approved, but not without the Trustees Treasurer commenting that the "system was not suited to existing conditions". The decision was carried 4 – 1. Pew lettings and rentals had been in practice in the downstairs area of Roscoe Place Chapel for many years. However, whilst a report to the Trustees' Meeting July 1918 states "that £66. 9s 0d was raised at a recent Anniversary", the Consolidated

Accounts for 1939 and 1940 show no income for pew rents in 1939 and only £11.5s 0d in 1940. Clearly the practice was going out of fashion at Roscoe Place.

By January 1935 the financial situation at Roscoe Place was such that a request was made for the annual assessment to be reduced, and the Circuit responded by lowering their assessment from £400 to £300 per year. At the same time the Leaders' Meeting Minutes for December 5th 1935 record a legacy given to Roscoe Trustees of over £1000 from the late Mr & Mrs Barnes. Yet, when the **Revd H. John Ivens** arrived to be minister for Roscoe Place in September 1939 he discovered that the Society was £500 in debt. The Annual Bazaar had been postponed but a Gift Day and Sale of Work was scheduled for 28th October. The Society Consolidated Accounts as reported to the Leaders' Meeting at 31st December 1940 show a church debt of £409.13s 5d! John Ivens appealed to the congregation about the finances and in his March Quarterly Letter 1941 states, "Finances suffer badly in winter-time. Collections one morning amounted to 6s 4d (and it cost over 30/- to heat the Chapel for that Service.)"

NEED FOR MISSION AND CRUSADE

In the inter-war years changes became evident in the membership at Roscoe Place. The Leaders' Meeting Minutes for September 1915 report a membership figure of 217 plus 9 "On trial"; 213 in March 1917; 216 in March 1923; 144 in December 1923; and 158 plus 14 "On trial" in January 1938 with 14 in the Junior Membership Class. What was happening in these years to bring about the sudden decrease in 1923 from 216 in March to 144 in December and the slow but gradual increase in the following years?

Dr Rupert E. Davies in his book entitled *Methodism* comments:

> "None of the Churches had even yet recovered from the shock of the First World War, and Methodism no more than any other. The men in the trenches, and the much smaller number of men who came home from the trenches, asked questions which the complacent but still dominant theology of the Victorian era was powerless to answer. The

gaps which appeared in once crowded churches were not all caused by the mass slaughter of the war."

Though Roscoe Place was able to continue a vigorous work among children, young people and young adults, was there reluctance on the part of an increasing number to become members of the Church? This implied a commitment which was being questioned more generally, and a financial obligation which was more difficult in the years of economic stringency.

The other important factor to take into consideration is that Roscoe Place Trustees at their January 1923 meeting "approved the principle of Methodist Union as set forth in the scheme by the Committee of the Three Churches concerned (i.e. Wesleyan Methodist, Primitive Methodist and the United Methodist Churches)." The Trustees voted: 11 For, 2 Against, and 2 Neutral. However, at their meeting in January 1925 the ten members present voted unanimously for the Union of Methodist Churches. Was this another issue having a bearing on who wished to remain members of Roscoe Place Wesleyan Chapel?

Whatever factors were involved in the changing pattern of membership at Roscoe Place, the need for a crusade or mission in the neighbourhood was implemented several times. In November 1931 the Revd Wilfred Gower with students (presumably from Headingley Wesleyan College) and local visitors carried out a mission. Another crusade in 1938 was conducted by the Revd H.W. Kenneth Sandy and two well-known evangelists, Mr Arthur Richards and the Revd George Allen. In his 1940 Christmas Quarterly Letter, John Ivens encouraged the formation of Home Fellowships – "gather a few neighbours in your home, sing hymns, read the Bible and pray together". Aggressive evangelism was being encouraged "to maintain a crusade spirit" and a letter of invitation was sent out to young people. In 1941 John Ivens again initiated an extensive visitation programme to be carried out with the help of leaders and visitors, and in 1945 the **Revd John C. Blackburn** and the Leaders' Meeting arranged for a 'commando campaign' to take place in December of that year.

It appears that as the years moved on between the two World Wars there was an increasing concern about the viability of Roscoe Place

Chapel in terms of membership and finance, and it would seem that Roscoe's stature in the Brunswick circuit was steadily declining. The consequences of WWI and the impact of WWII appear to have put a strain on the spiritual resources of Roscoe which were difficult to offset.

However, during the Second World War years a great deal of fellowship activity and money raising endeavours took place with the determination of keeping Roscoe Place alive. The August 1941 Leaders' Meeting minutes indicate a very active church life with Sunday School, Boys' Brigade and Life Boys, Sisterhood, Missionary Society, Women's Work and Juvenile Missions, Girl Guides, Junior Choir, Chapel Choir, Sunshine Band, Youth Circle and a Temperance Book.

The Minute Book records the continuing involvement of these groups through to1945 but with no mention of the Wesley Guild! Perhaps the early 'straw in the wind' is found in the report to the Leaders' Meeting of February 1930 that "the Wesley Guild had an average attendance of 14 and slight progress was being made". By the beginning of WWII the Wesley Guild at Roscoe Place seems to have dropped out of sight even though the Movement started at this Church in 1896 and has world-wide outreach to this day!

Leeds 13th Life Boys Section 1930-31
NB Harry Cocksedge, Officer in Charge

Leeds 13th Boys' Brigade Company 1930-31

REMINISCENCES TWO
— POST-WINDRUSH

ROSCOE and US

WEST INDIANS WERE ARRIVING in England in large numbers (in the 1950s) including myself. We came to the so called "mother" country to help rebuild the damage the country had suffered during Second World War. When we arrived we came with enthusiasm and optimism but that quickly disappeared. The people here in Yorkshire at the time were not very welcoming nor friendly towards us apart from a few members of the local community. We had great difficulty in finding a place to live, work, to socialise and even a place of worship. The only church that showed any compassion, warmth and respect towards us was Roscoe (Place) Methodist Church.

An insurance agent called Mr Mulligan would visit and encourage us to take out insurance and also help us with any problem we encountered. A minister by the name of Reverend Harry Salmon would come and visit us in our homes (bedsit) to check on our well being, offer support and to pray with us. A few other families, Lunns, Cocksedges, Elsie (Plumb) and Valerie (Atkinson) helped us set up The West Indian Fellowship where we sang hymns, read scriptures and had tea and biscuits together.

On Bank Holidays Mr Lunn would organise trips to holiday resorts such as seasides, stately homes, parks, castles, Coventry Cathedral and Gretna Green (where couples were married over the anvil). Roscoe Church noticed how much we loved cricket so they went about setting up a West Indian cricket team which I was made captain of. We managed to get our own pitch at Roundhay Park. This was very successful, our matches attracted large crowds and at one particular match in Garforth the opposition had an Ex-England player Jony Wardle. WE GAVE THEM A THRASHING!!!

As my relationship grew stronger with the church I was appointed as the first black Society Steward. This was a position I felt very proud of and it had a great impact on me and the West Indian community.

Roscoe's hospitality and warmth reached members of other Christian denominations like Enos Harris who was a Church of England member and went to St Clements' Church, where his membership was rejected because of the colour of his skin He then joined Roscoe Church where he became a choirmaster and an upright member until his death.

Roscoe Methodist Church did not just give warmth: it also accommodated anyone regardless of their religious background to perform marriages, burials, christenings and blessings. Our ministers have attended other churches to perform wedding ceremonies and funeral prayers. If you check the old church records we had 13 baptisms in one service which was the highest number recorded.

Arthur France MBE

(NB MV Empire Windrush arrived at Tilbury docks on the 22nd June 1948 bringing 492 passengers from Jamaica. This is reckoned as the beginning of the steady flow of West Indian immigrants to England/UK)

MEMORIES OF THE OLD ROSCOE
Allan Herbert

I FIRST CAME TO ROSCOE METHODIST CHURCH in September 1955 from Charlestown, Nevis. At that time, people from the Caribbean were not welcomed at all churches, but Roscoe was a warm and friendly place of worship and welcomed everyone. Soon, most if not all of the growing black community were worshiping there and became members. The Revd Harry Salmon was the preacher at the time and you would often open your front door to find him paying you a visit. Evening services were well attended and were followed by an Anglo-West Indian Fellowship in the Church Hall, which was across the yard. This fellowship would be led by a different member each Sunday evening and we would sing hymns and worship as we did in the Caribbean.

Morning services were not as well attended. On the first Sunday of the month there would be the Order of Morning Service but the Te Deum etc were sung and not read as it is today. Roscoe had the 13th Leeds

Boys' Brigade and once a month the Band would parade around the local streets. The Brigade eventually folded but was restarted by the Rev Trevor Bates at the new Roscoe. Sunday School started at 2.30 pm and was held in the Church Hall across the yard. Ministers in training at Headingley were attached to Roscoe and the Revd Glendinning and the Revd Bostock were two of these. They would visit families and would be invited to have a Caribbean style Sunday dinner with them, familiarising themselves with the different foods of the Caribbean.

The old Roscoe was a big church built in the tradition of its day, with beautiful stained glass windows and upstairs balconies. However, in order for it to be warm on Sunday mornings, the coal-fired boiler would have to be lit on Saturday morning. Unfortunately, as the houses around Roscoe were demolished, the church was broken into frequently and items, especially those made of lead, would disappear. The roof suffered constantly. As Property Steward, I was called regularly to sort out the repairs.

On the social side, there would be Social Evenings some Saturday nights and these were always well attended. Day trips would be organised by Mr R Lunn and I can recall going to places like New Brighton and Trentham Gardens, but the most memorable trip of all was the one when we stopped off at Gretna Green and a mock wedding Over the Anvil took place between Ms E Plumb and Mr A France. (We still have a photograph of this event). There were always three young ladies sitting at the back of the coach - Elsie, Barbara and Valerie – and they would lead the sing-song all the way home, not forgetting to sing "On Ilkley Moor" and "Valarie Valarye". There would be an annual trip to Garforth where Roscoe Cricket team would challenge Garforth Methodist Church's Cricket team to a match. Roscoe would always win, of course. The match would then be followed by afternoon tea. An annual Dinner would .take place in the Church Hall but in the last years this was moved to the Capital Ballroom at Meanwood.

As time went by, membership dwindled as members moved on to start their own churches or reverted back to the religion they followed in the Caribbean. The ones who remained became the backbone of Roscoe Methodist Church, taking on the various roles within the church.

(Compiled by Allan's daughter Adora Maynard)

40

HAPPY MEMORIES OF ROSCOE METHODIST CHURCH

I ARRIVED IN BIRMINGHAM in 1956 and came to Leeds, where I knew someone, a few weeks later, in order to find employment. I attended Roscoe Place Methodist Church, the original building, where I was welcomed by the Revd Harry Salmon and his successor the Revd Russell Moston.

On my behalf, the Revd Salmon contacted one of his friends, Mr Johnson, who had an engineering business and asked him to employ me. Mr Johnson was a senior steward at Victoria Methodist Church, Victoria Road, Hyde Park, Leeds 6 (now Bethel Church).

I remained with this company, Johnson Bros., for three years and became a part of their family. Some outside jobs could not be done because of the winter and some workers had to be laid off. I found another job where I stayed for many years.

I loved Roscoe Place Methodist Church and attended both the morning and evening services. Many West Indians were warmly welcomed here, not only by the ministers, but also by many members of the church. Mr & Mrs Roland Lunn and their daughter Dorothy looked after us as part of their family. Elsie Plumb was also a very good friend.

With other members, I became involved with special plays which were organised and presented by the Revd Kenneth Glendinning. I also became a church steward and a member of the choir. The organist was Mr Leslie Farnill.

We decided to restart the Steel Band at the present Roscoe Church and I became a bass player, but after developing a painful knee I had to leave the band. I remain a loyal member of Roscoe and get involved in as many aspects of the church life as I can.

Elbert Moving

41

MEMORIES OF OLD AND NEW ROSCOE

A MIXED GROUP of us from St Kitts came to Leeds on January 13th 1955, and eventually found accommodation in Chapeltown. The next day we were visited by Mr Perkins, the Probationer Minister of Roscoe Place Methodist Church, Chapeltown Road. He said that the minister there was the Revd Harry Salmon. These ministers were kind to us. Within the week, they got us registered with the local general practitioners and also got us into jobs. We were very grateful.

Norman, one of the members of Roscoe Place used to collect our children to take them to Sunday School. Eventually we started to attend the morning service, and got to know Mr & Mrs Roland Lunn and their daughter Dorothy. They were kind to newcomers.

The church was traditional and lively, so we soon settled there. After the evening service, the Anglo West Indian Fellowship met to pray and sing favourite hymns and choruses for spiritual upliftment. To raise money to build the present Roscoe Methodist Church, I remember taking a letter to my work to ask colleague to buy a brick. I had a very good response. It was pleasing to see the building completed.

Our family continued to worship there. Our daughter Vera became a Sunday School Teacher and my wife Constancia was a loyal member of the Women's Fellowship and other committees.

I WILL NEVER FORGET ROSCOE

Hilton Pitt (1955 onwards)

Chapter Three
NEW DIRECTIONS
1946 – 1962

It is important to bear in mind the changing residential patterns in the housing of Chapeltown at this time. By the 1930s the housing in the Louis Street, Leopold Street and Francis Street area was being occupied by aspiring Jewish and Irish people who had larger families; the previous master and servant households were moving out of Chapeltown to the Chapel Allerton, Moortown and Alwoodley areas. In 1936 The Holy Rosary Roman Catholic Church was built on the corner of Louis Street and Chapeltown Road, obviously to meet the needs of a growing Irish community in this neighbourhood. Clearly Chapeltown was becoming a transitional area for immigrant people.

We believe that the first **Roscoe Place Methodist Manse** was at No.6 Louis Street. Certainly by September 1871 the Roscoe minister was at that address. However, in an advert in the Bradford Observer (March 12th 1863) Lockwood & Mawson architects of Leeds & Bradford were seeking quotations for the building of a minister's house at Roscoe Place. Whether this was at No.6 Louis Street or rather the Caretaker's residence adjacent to the Roscoe Place Chapel, at the rear, is unclear. By the 1930s however, the circuit decided to move the Manse to Oak Road, and then eventually in the 1960s to Gledhow Park Road where it is to this day. This seems to reflect the changing nature of the housing situation and conditions in Chapeltown across the century. So we cannot doubt that Roscoe Place Methodist Church was being influenced by these changes both in its membership and in its ministry.

It would be easy to assume that Roscoe's congregation was beginning to falter by the end of World War II due to concerns about membership and finance. However, **Doreen Warman** (*nee Doreen Allison, second daughter of Revd Lewis H. Allison, minister at Roscoe Place 1946-52) (see Appendix)* recalls one moment of encouragement experienced by her father:

> 'He told of how on one Gift Day occasion a member who lived in Roundhay came to him and said she had just had new carpets

43

fitted in her home. (Revd Lewis Allison then began to think that this lady would go on to say "therefore I will not be able to give to the Gift Day this year") However, she had decided to give double the amount she usually gave as a Thank Offering!' WOW!

There is clear alternative evidence of vitality at Roscoe Place in Doreen's 'Reminiscences' *(see Appendix)*. Doreen, who was a teenager during those years, and involved with the Youth activities of Roscoe, writes: "Roscoe at this time was certainly a lively church, full of activity". Doreen continues to say:

> "It was the immediate post-war era. During the war the churches had been denuded of their men folk – families had been split by evacuation, and relatives in different parts of the country were looking after their children...The churches were beginning to pick up. The Methodist Church was foremost at this time with a mission to reach young people, with its strong and inspiring leadership from the Methodist Youth Department."

WORK AMONG CHILDREN AND YOUNG PEOPLE– POST WORLD WAR II

During the time when Lewis H. Allison was minister for Roscoe Place Chapel in the Brunswick circuit, work among children and young people was seemingly strong and vigorous. The **13th Boys' Brigade Company** in the 1950/51 Session still had 30 boys with 10 officers! They won six Battalion awards including the Senior Band Mace, and they had a Silver Band of 15 boys with 3 officers! Doreen Warman comments:

> "The 13th Leeds BB was a legend in the area. It had a good, strong leadership team of totally committed leaders, some of whom were church stewards...On monthly Parade Sundays the brigade paraded round the streets led by its band, always drawing crowds to listen to the band, and watch the mace bearer spectacularly throw up, and miraculously catch the mace!"

The **Girl Guide Company** 20 years after being started, was very robust. **Miss Joyce Reyner**, their Captain, was also District Commissioner. 'Guides from this Company were enabled to go camping with the District Guides, helping to develop their full potential'. Doreen Warman reports that a **Rangers Section** for the Roscoe Guide Company was started during her time, led by **Mrs Doris Lythe**. Doris also helped to create a **Young People's Discussion Group**, studying the Bible in depth, which in turn became the basis for a **Membership Group**, and also a **Youth Mission Team** which took services around the circuit. Lewis Allison was passionate about youth work and he started a **Youth Club** which became very successful. Again Doreen Warman remembers "seeing the large hall full of young people involved in various activities. Table Tennis, snooker, darts, arts and crafts, learning ballroom dancing were some of the activities." Some of the young people attended **MAYC** (*Methodist Association of Youth Clubs*) **London Weekends** and **Methodist Youth Camps**.

In those years lay leadership was strong. **Arthur and Elsie Firth, Frank and Elsie Farrar, Elsie and Gladys Ackroyd, the Boyle family, Mabel Tate and Irene Vickers**, not to mention **Eileen Gaunt**, were all part of the extremely able and involved group of men and women who were totally committed to the life of Roscoe Place in spite of many changes.

OVERSEAS MISSIONS

Benjamin Randall Vickers tells us that he was present at the meeting in Leeds (Old Boggart Chapel) when the Wesleyan Missionary Society was first started in 1813 and he would have been 15 years old. A lively interest in the work of Overseas Missions across the years at Roscoe Place may well have found its encouragement in that experience! Couple it with the fact that two families – **Vickers** and **Simpson** of Roscoe Place - had members who served in overseas missionary work in Burma and China early in the twentieth century would also help to explain the continued enthusiasm!

In the Benjamin Randall Vickers family – **Agnes Vickers** sister of William Farrar Vickers went to Mandalay, Burma in 1898, and in 1907 married Revd Will Vickery, an Irish Methodist minister in Burma, where they remained until returning to England in 1921. Her sister **Helen Vickers**, married Dr. George Hadden, also Irish, and went as a doctor to China. Farrar's brother **Dr B Randall Vickers** married Mabel Gurney and went to Hong Kong 1911 – 1917. After a year in the Medical Corps he returned to China in 1919 and served in Chuchow until 1924.

In the Simpson family – **Barbara Simpson** youngest sister of **Doris** (*who married William Farrar Vickers*) went as a missionary to China in 1920 and served for thirty eight years. On her return to this country was a guiding influence in Methodist Missionary policy and support.

We have already mentioned The **Revd William Threlfall** of Hollowforth, Preston. He was an older brother of Margaret who married Benjamin Randall Vickers in 1836. William's story (*See Chapter One*) was also an early inspiration for the Roscoe Place congregation to work for Overseas Missions because of the connection with Margaret Vickers.

We are not surprised to learn that **Eileen Gaunt**, who was Brown Owl for the Brownies and JMA (*Junior Missionary Association*) secretary at Roscoe Place, gained a strong call to work overseas during her early years at Roscoe. Only after the death of her parents was she free to offer for the Deaconess Order. Eileen entered the Deaconess Training College at Ilkley in 1950, and was ordained as a Deaconess in 1954. After five years serving in England she offered for work overseas and sailed for the West Indies in 1959, working in Jamaica and Guyana. After ten years Eileen returned to work in England until her retirement in 1980 when she returned to live in Chapeltown and remained a dedicated member with Roscoe Methodist Church until her death in 1996.

"The tradition of strong support for Overseas Missions at Roscoe Place was encouraged annually by the Brunswick Circuit Overseas Missions Weeks just after WWII, when four returned missionaries would arrive in the circuit to be introduced and then take special services and meetings around the circuit." **Doreen Warman** attributes her own sense of call to work overseas to that influence. This culminated in marrying the Revd Noel Warman in Accra, Ghana in 1960.

Little did the Roscoe Place congregation know in those early years that a new future was to unfold for their Church in Chapeltown when Caribbean people would carry on the proud tradition of Roscoe into the 21st Century! Doreen Warman says, "Perhaps the 'straw in the wind' heralding the dramatic change was the arrival at Roscoe Place Chapel one Sunday morning in 1947 of two West African students from the Gold Coast (*later Ghana*) who were studying in Leeds.. They were **Dan Brown** and **Quafo Manti**. At a time when it was unusual to see coloured people they were received with a warm welcome and generous hospitality. Roscoe Place friends invited them into their homes, and during their stay in Leeds remained at Roscoe Place." In 1960 Doreen met both of them again in Ghana when by that time Quafo Manti was a doctor, and Dan Brown was the General Manager of Ghana's one thousand government run schools!

A TURNING POINT IN THE LIFE OF ROSCOE PLACE

In **September 1954** the **Revd Harry Salmon**, newly married, and just out of Wesley College, Headingley was stationed in the Brunswick circuit with responsibility for Roscoe Place Church. Harry remained for four years until 1958. In his "Reminiscences" (*see Appendix*) he comments:

> "On his first Sunday at Roscoe the congregations were small in that very large old church. What was unusual for those days, was the presence of black faces as well as white faces in both morning and evening congregations. In the morning there were two Boys' Brigade members from Jamaica attending an international BB gathering. In the evening there was a couple who had recently arrived as immigrants from the West Indies. I mention this because it marked a turning point in the long history of Roscoe Place. At a personal level, it also greatly influenced the course of my ministry."

During the coming months and years Harry and the Roscoe Place folks were to witness a steady stream of people arriving in Chapeltown from the West Indies. Very many of them were Methodists who came from the islands of Nevis and St.Kitts in the Leeward Islands. In the 1950s these Caribbean people arriving and looking for work in Leeds were

47

being accommodated in rented rooms and flats in the larger houses of Chapeltown. The owners had moved out of the community but retained control of the properties they vacated, charging high rents. The overcrowding which resulted produced unacceptable housing conditions for a people living in completely new, strange, and distressing circumstances.

Harry Salmon, with the Roscoe Place folk initiated a visitation programme, based on lists of names and addresses compiled by him on the basis of information from relatives and friends in the growing West Indian community in Chapeltown.

However, because the visitation programme became so important in helping to care for newly arrived West Indians Harry appealed to Wesley College students to help Roscoe Place with this new venture in ministry. The key person in this student group was **J.Russell Moston** (*later Revd and minister of Roscoe following Harry Salmon*). Russell Moston's diary about this work began in the latter months of 1954 and tells of the difficulties in trying to find and visit people at home and of the miserable living conditions, often without adequate heating. Russell gave much of his spare time whilst at College in helping in this work, particularly at weekends. He also mentions travelling by tram up Chapeltown Road to get to Harehills Avenue to do visiting.

Additional help also arrived in 1955 when the **Lincoln Fields Methodist Chapel** had to close and 'most of their few members joined up with Roscoe.' These included the Lunn family (*Roland, Sarah and Dorothy*), Elsie Plumb and Jessie Peacock. 'They enthusiastically joined in the life of their "new" church.' Harry Salmon asked Roland Lunn to become Sunday School Superintendent, and he agreed. Roscoe Place was now about to cross a new threshold into a completely different world from the one it was leaving behind and by November 1955 Harry Salmon was referring to Roscoe Place as an "Anglo-West Indian" Church.

Within weeks of Harry being minister at Roscoe West Indians began to attend worship at Roscoe Place, and gradually Roscoe became known among Caribbean people in the wider community as the 'Church with a warm welcome' for them. Russell Moston's diary entry for Saturday and Sunday 20/21st November 1954 tells of how after a lot of visiting on the Saturday when he had experienced 'being misunderstood and openly rejected,' he realised how much he needed God's help to enable him to carry on. After further visitation on the Sunday (this time dressed with a clerical collar!) he received a more positive response in his visiting and at the evening service there were 'eight coloured people present' and he was 'overjoyed that evening for a wonderful day'!

PASTORAL WORK AND COMMUNITY CONCERN

It is difficult to realise now just how much Harry Salmon and Russell Moston were caught up in a rapidly changing pattern of involvement with an increasing West Indian population in Chapeltown, with all the pastoral, domestic and social problems which ensued. The dedicated and sacrificial concern for the people from both of them was shared by a few loyal laymen. The Manse at Oak Road became a hub of activity offering welcome, hospitality, advice and support for those new arrivals who were feeling lost and overwhelmed in their new setting.

At Roscoe Place Russell Moston sensed the need to start a fellowship meeting on Saturday evenings. This began in February 1955 and, along with the encouragement for West Indians to worship at Roscoe Place on Sundays helped to change the composition of the Roscoe Place Sunday congregations. By July 1955 there were 12 West Indians attending Sunday Services, and notes Russell, 'on the 1st August there were 29 West Indians at the Saturday evening Fellowship, and at the Sunday Services 27 English people and 29 West Indians'! On Sunday November 13th 1955 Harry Salmon conducted a special 'Anglo-West Indian Service' on the theme "For Better, For Worse". 'There were 210 West Indians at the service, with 100 West Indians and a good number of English people at the Fellowship'! There could be no turning back or turning away from what seemed to be the clear guidance of God!

The **Aggrey Society Social Club** started in 1955 was holding its meetings at their Club Room, 79 Spencer Place, Leeds 7 and was available to immigrant people in Chapeltown. This was one of the first ventures to cater specially for 'coloured people' in that neighbourhood.. A 'Host Members Rota Attendance' for January to March 1956 shows that Roland Lunn was one of 27 Europeans and 27 West Indians and

Asians who shared in this hosting task for the Club open every evening 8 – 10pm. This was a venture strongly supported by both Russell Moston and Harry Salmon.

Housing provision and conditions for immigrants were a matter of high priority concern for a number of people in Leeds, including Harry Salmon and **Mr J.C. Charlesworth**, a solicitor of Leeds who specialised in Housing Law and who took the initiative with others to form the **Aggrey Housing Society** in 1955. It was evident that West Indians were not being given any consideration or priority by the local authority when there was a crying need. By the end of the 1960s a hundred West Indians were being accommodated in properties newly acquired by the Aggrey Housing Society offering better conditions at fairer rents. In the 1960s Revd Malcolm Furness strongly campaigned for investment in the Aggrey Housing Society, and raised £15,000 in this way. In 1977 Aggrey Housing Society amalgamated with Yorkshire Cottage Housing Association Ltd and was later absorbed into the Leeds and Yorkshire Housing Association Ltd.

THE BURDEN OF CHURCH PROPERTY MAINTENANCE

In those years of Harry Salmon's ministry there was a steady movement by many of the 'traditional members' of Roscoe Place to move residence into the Chapel Allerton area and beyond. Some retained their connections with Roscoe whilst others transferred to nearer churches, and this had a real impact on Roscoe's weekly income. In 1956 a special leaflet was issued to members of Roscoe Place appealing for more realistic giving and inviting them to join the Envelope System. It stated among other things:

> "During 1955 the income from Sunday Collection averaged only £8 per week. We had to have special efforts to bridge the gap between income and expenditure. Last year on an average £4 per week was spent on fuel and lighting."

At the same time Roscoe's large property was becoming increasingly difficult to maintain because of its age and the financial costs involved. Harry states:

"During this time the church spire became unsafe (*almost 100 years old*), and part of it had to be removed at considerable cost. Fortunately one of our fine members who was also a trustee and was involved in the building industry (*probably Mr Arthur Firth*) was able to guide us through a difficult period at minimum cost. This explained why for its last days Roscoe Place had a flat 'spire'!"

The high priority which Harry Salmon gave to working with Caribbean people in Chapeltown, and particularly those from St Kitts and Nevis resulted in more and more West Indians of various denominations attending both worship and the **Anglo-West Indian Fellowship** on Sundays. Hymn-singing was robust and 'the life of Roscoe was enriched by the presence of vibrant and enthusiastic Christians'. Baptism became a feature of morning services and often on a Saturday there would be several weddings In the Methodist Conference (*held in Leeds*) Handbook for 1956 Harry is reported as saying: "In December (*1955*) we had thirty-four West Indian members and five On Trial. The Church has been enriched by this partnership in God's work" (*at Roscoe Place*). The atmosphere of Caribbean worship was being transplanted to an English setting!

New direction for the Roscoe Place congregation had finally set in. This was due to the magnificent work done by Harry and Greta Salmon with the help of J. Russell Moston and students from Wesley College, Headingley together with a dedicated group of West Indians and English folk. **Dr. James E. Kwegyir Aggrey** (*1875-1927*) of the Gold Coast, West Africa had become well-known for proclaiming (*after his experiences of prejudice in the USA*) for proclaiming that, just as we need the black and white keys of a piano to create harmony so, likewise, black and white people living and working together could create harmony in society. This allegory was not only the motto for the **Aggrey Society** in Chapeltown but it was also being illustrated by the new congregations of Roscoe Place from the 1950s.

THE NEXT STAGE

In 1958 Harry Salmon moved on and the **Revd J. Russell Moston** was selected to return to Leeds and become Roscoe's minister. Russell

51

having been in at the beginning of the changes at Roscoe Place, shared the original vision and so was able to continue the transformation work at Roscoe helping to save Roscoe Place from being a dying cause. Russell also recalls a 'growing number of Weddings when I first returned to Roscoe Place. Sometimes as many as four on a Saturday!' He also remembers one Sunday morning when there were 20 Baptisms!

Russell recalls:
> "The 'Old Roscoe' was used in the early days by the 'upper class' of Chapeltown. Every pew had a card with the name of the family who 'rented it'. The 'servants' had to sit in the gallery only. It was frequently visited by Army Officers, who were from the local garrison ... When I arrived as Minister in 1958, I removed the old and very dusty name tags from the pews – only to find that one or two had been replaced by new 'tags' by the next Sunday!"

Russell Moston picked up his former connections with the **Leeds International Council** (*1955*), with the Aggrey Society (*1955*) and with the **Leeds Council for Social Services,** supporting the endeavours being made to improve the housing provision and work opportunities. He maintained Roscoe Place's priority to care for West Indian immigrants. **Mary Stratton** of the Leeds Council of Social Services invited him to be the Chair of the Study Group "Employment & Social Welfare of Coloured People" in 1959, part of a nationwide study to report to the British National Conference of Social Services.

Russell's ministry based on Roscoe Place had a double emphasis: to seek to build up and stabilise the congregational life at Roscoe and to maintain contacts and involvement in the wider community for the good of all concerned, especially Caribbean people in Chapeltown. Roscoe still had its Boys' Brigade and Life Boys; Girl Guides and Brownies. There was also a substantial work among womenfolk: a Women's Fellowship meeting; a separate Women's Work meeting (*supporting missionary work overseas*) and a Sunshine Band with regular Tea Meetings. Eventually the Women's Work meeting and the Monday Women's Fellowship united to become one meeting.

REMINISCENCES THREE

MY EARLY DAYS AT ROSCOE

"For God has not given us the spirit of fear, but of power, and of love, and of a sound mind" (2 Tim.1:7)

I WAS BORN in Nevis and lived in St Kitts for 5 years. In 1959 after sailing for 17 days, I arrived in England. My ultimate destination was Leeds, to rejoin my sister Muriel, who lived at 9 Amberley Grove, Leeds 7. On the first Sunday after my arrival, despite the snow, I wanted to attend church, and I was directed to the nearest, Roscoe Place Methodist. I attended evening service and I was surprised that only five of us were in the congregation. This was a disappointment, when compared to the large congregation in St Kitts and Nevis. I renewed friendship with people I knew from "home" and eventually became friends with members and others who lived in the community. The following Sunday, I was welcomed by the minister Reverend Moston, Mr & Mrs Lunn, Mr & Mrs Cocksedge, Mr & Mrs Harrison and many others. The service was different from what I was used to and not as vibrant. Over a period of time the West Indian members were able to influence the format of the worship.

I very soon became involved in many areas of Roscoe Church's life – stewardship, the choir and Sunday School. I felt fulfilled in serving Roscoe, old and new.

In 1962 I was married at Roscoe to Ulrica Eastman from Barbados, a student nurse. We had three children, who were christened at Roscoe. Our son Andrew, represented Roscoe on an Overseas Youth Exchange visit, within the Methodist Church.

The ministers and members of Roscoe encouraged me to move forward in all areas of my life. Reverend Trevor Bates in particular, boosted my confidence, and I became a local councillor in 1980 representing Chapel Allerton Ward, a magistrate and Methodist preacher On Trial. As a local councillor, I did overseas visits to represent the city of Leeds.

Being a member of Roscoe made me happy to serve, together with all the ministers and members of Roscoe old and new.

As Charles Wesley wrote…
To serve the present age
My calling to fulfil
O may it all my powers engage
To do my master's will

Cedric Clarke

THE EUBANKS FAMILY

MY NAME IS SADIE EUBANKS and I have a very long association with Roscoe Methodist Church

I came to England from Jamaica in 1956 and stayed with my brother in Leeds. After settling down in Leeds I started to attend Roscoe Methodist Church at its old site in Sheepscar and with its mixed congregation I was made very welcome and felt at home. I got married to George early in 1957 and he too began to worship at Roscoe. We were now regulars and it was not long before we were regularly visited by Mr Lunn and Mr Arthur France encouraging us to become members.

We not only became members, we also played a part in being involved at the new site, where the church was rebuilt on Francis Street. My duties included not only being a member of the church, but also being a member of WIFCOS, a Welcoming Steward and a Choir member, whilst my husband George became very active with the then minister, Revd Trevor Bates. His duties included being a Steward, Property Steward, Church Secretary, Captain of the Boys' Brigade, Sunday School teacher and he also attended Synod meetings. Roscoe gave my husband George an overwhelming send off when he passed away. Although he died in Jamaica, his heart was always at the Church and when a memorial service was organised for him £450 was collected, which was sent to the Church he was an Elder at in Jamaica, to help with repairs after hurricane damage.

54

George and I had two children – Paul and Diane. Paul helped to raise money for Roscoe and in the 1980s he organised a very successful comedy show. Paul also played a part in running the Boys' Brigade football team and for a short time worked with Mrs Mary Saddler as part of the WIFCOS team.

Diane also attended Sunday School and Church. She was a member of the Girls' Brigade and was proud to be a JMA collector.

I have nothing but praise for Roscoe Methodist Church and the way we as a congregation look after one another. Our minister Mark is always there for us and with his enthusiasm we are still raising money towards the upkeep of 'our' church.

Sadie, Paul and Diane Eubanks

OLD ROSCOE PLACE CHAPEL

THE CHURCH WAS OPENED in 1862 and in 1894 the Wesley Guild was formed by the minister of the church, Reverend W.B. Fitzgerald. Another highlight is that in 1914 it was known as the garrison church, due to the barracks in Barrack Road.

Before we came to Roscoe Place Methodist Church we used to worship at the Lincoln Fields Chapel until it closed in 1955. We didn't know to which next church we would be going, but in January 1955, I was in St James's Hospital when the minister of the old Roscoe Place Methodist Church, Reverend Harry Salmon, came in to visit a patient from Ashley Road Methodist Church who was in the next bed to me. Revd Salmon got talking to me and the outcome of this talk was, that he asked me if I would be willing to become the General Superintendent of the Roscoe Place Sunday School.

We did not know why we were sent to Roscoe but, at that time the West Indian friends were coming over here and on Sunday evenings after church the Anglo-West Indian Fellowship Meeting took place and was attended by 50 or 60 people. In those days, Revd Salmon used to walk the streets and would speak to all the West Indians he met and invite them to church.

The Centenary celebration took place in 1962 when a special cake was made for the church. HAPPY DAYS!

Roland Lunn

FROM DOROTHY LUNN

I CAME TO ROSCOE PLACE METHODIST CHURCH when I was 11 years old with my mother and father in 1955, when the black people came into the church. I went to the Sunday School on a Sunday afternoon, and went to church in the morning and at night.

When I was older I came to be a Sunday School teacher, and I was in the Girl Guides. I came to be a Life Boy leader with Valerie Atkinson and Graham Glover, who were leaders. When we went to the new Church I was a Girls' Brigade leader and a Class Leader in the Church.

Dorothy Lunn

I REMEMBER – ROSCOE CHURCH FROM THE 1960s

ROSCOE CHURCH in the 1960s had, as part of its function, activities for the young and the poor in the community.

Mrs Phillip confirmed that Mr Kenneth Glendinning was a minister in Roscoe and he was involved with the youth. He ran the Youth Club every Thursday. There was the Boys' Brigade and the Girl Guides – all initiated by the Church. This function would also appear to have helped with integrating the influx of West Indians into the Chapeltown Community.

"I emigrated to Leeds in the late 1950s", she said. In those days it was traditional for most West Indians to attend Church and they would take their children with them, thus planting the seed. I attended Roscoe Church. It was a big stone church at the bottom of Chapeltown Road. Mr Glendinning and I became good friends as we were involved in other activities in the community. I subsequently taught children in Sunday School at Roscoe Church in the seventies.

Jane Tuckett on behalf of
Mrs Diana Phillip JP NNEB AMRSH (1927-2011)

56

Chapter Four
TRANSFORMATION CONTINUES
1962-1974

Russell Moston moved on in 1962 and the **Revd J. Malcolm Furness** was stationed in the Brunswick circuit to be the minister for Roscoe Place. During Malcolm's time the Brunswick Circuit was divided and Roscoe Place became part of the new Leeds Chapel Allerton Circuit (*later Leeds North East*). putting it in a wider fellowship of churches. Malcolm writes (*see his 'Reminiscences' in Appendix*):

> "The Church we came to was a busy, vibrant community where something was happening every day – B.B., Youth Club, Church Fellowship, Vestry Hour, Women's Fellowship, and the Sunday congregation was a healthy mixture of white, black and brown – West Indian, African and native English. Later we welcomed a Cypriot, a Hungarian and an Indian doctor to our multi-racial flock."

The extraordinary ministry which evolved over nearly two decades (*1954 – 72*), implemented by the ministers of those years, made a considerable impact upon the community of Chapeltown and became a lifeline of hope for Caribbean people living there. Indeed, we dare to claim that Roscoe Place Methodist Church was pioneering a new way of integration and acceptance which the whole city of Leeds would learn from. Malcolm Furness in an interview for '**Kingdom Overseas**' (*the Methodist Overseas Missions magazine*) states that "we are encouraging West Indians to become leaders in the church at Roscoe Place alongside white people".

A clear illustration of this is in the fact that several West Indians who were members at Roscoe Place were willing to accept the responsibility of leadership. Within fifteen months of Malcolm Furness being with Roscoe Place **Mrs Evangeline Buchanan, Mr Arthur France, Mr Allan Herbert, Mr Enos Harris, Mr Arthur Saddler** and **Mrs Myrna Tyrell** were all appointed members of the Leaders' Meeting. In 1964 **Mr Allan Herbert** became the first of the West Indian Class Leaders and, along with **Mr Elbert Moving**, became a Poor Steward.

57

In 1965 **Mr Andrew Nelson** became Captain of the 13th BB Company, **Mr Arthur France** and **Mr Elbert Moving** were made Society Stewards, **Mrs Myrna Tyrell** became Secretary for Overseas Missions and, in 1966, **Mr John Connor** became Superintendent of the Junior Dept. of the Sunday School. As the composition of the congregation began to change over the following years, so also did the share in leadership of Roscoe increase among the West Indian members. By 1969 **Mrs Lilian Byam** had also become a Class Leader.

Malcolm Furness realised the importance of encouraging the Caribbean members of Roscoe Place Chapel to share in the task of being responsible for the running and maintenance of the church. Yet the pastoral oversight and visitation of people was borne by and large by himself, along with one or two West Indian volunteers and the 14 Class Leaders, the majority of whom were not of Caribbean origin. The reasons are not hard to find. Most West Indian folk had to try and find work wherever they could, and so often that was with occupations which involved shift-work or unsocial hours making it quite impossible for them to find the spare time to be Pastoral Visitors.

One of the distinctive features introduced and continued through the 1960s was the observance of **Emancipation Sunday – the first Sunday in August**. This was an opportunity to celebrate the end of slavery in the British West Indies in 1834, emphasizing the dignity and full humanity of black people. Usually the guest preacher on these occasions was a Methodist minister who had served in the Caribbean. The Revd William Sunter *(former Chairman of the Leeward Islands District, who in his retirement years lived in West Yorkshire)* was treated as a special guest on these occasions. In addition to this special Sunday the Order for Morning Prayer was introduced on a regular basis *(monthly)* because the folk from the Caribbean were used to this form of worship in their home churches.

LEEWARD ISLANDS CONFLICT MEETING

On September 5th 1967 a crisis event took place at Roscoe Place involving Malcolm Furness which was reported in both the *Yorkshire Post* and the *Yorkshire Evening Post* the next day under the headlines:

"Minister bans politics in his church" and "West Indian politics in a Leeds church hall":

"An English Methodist minister appealed for order – when 400 West Indians packed a hall at Roscoe Methodist Church, Chapeltown Road ... the Revd J. Malcolm Furness, minister of the church, made his appeal during a noisy interruption of a speech by Mr Fitzroy Briant, Minister of Education, Health and Welfare for the Caribbean islands of St Kitts Nevis and Anguilla. Mr Briant's speech followed a long explanation by Mr Robert Bradshaw, Premier of the newly independent three-island state, of events surrounding an armed insurrection and a bid for the independence of Anguilla ... (on May 30th 1967)

"Later, while Mr Briant was speaking, Mr Furness rose to check an outburst of laughter. He appealed from the platform that there should be no political discussion ... My church does not permit such discussions inside its buildings and I ask you to observe this' ... He told the meeting that discourtesy had been done not to himself but to his Church ... But Mr Furness was shouted down."

"Mr Bradshaw later apologised to Mr Furness for any discourtesy shown to him or his Church"

This event seems to have been arranged by the United Caribbean Association with the request to use Roscoe Place Church Hall for a private meeting and for Malcolm Furness to be the Chairperson. The event highlights very clearly the strong links between West Indians from St Kitts Nevis and Anguilla in Leeds and their home islands. It also underlines the fact that by 1967 Roscoe Place Methodist Church was clearly identified with West Indian folk in Chapeltown so that seemed right for the organisers of the meeting to approach Malcolm Furness with the request that it might take place there.

ADDITIONAL STAFFING FOR INNER-CITY WORK

By 1964 it became evident to the Brunswick Circuit that the work in the inner-city section, mainly Chapeltown and Harehills, was presenting such opportunities for ministry and growth of the Church's work that Malcolm Furness should have an assistant. In **September 1965**, with the financial help of a Connexional Home Mission grant, the **Revd D. Gerald Bostock** was stationed as a probationer minister in the circuit, working alongside Malcolm and remained until August 1967.

Gerald, in addition to regular visiting of members and families connected with Roscoe Place, was able to give more time to work among children and young people connected with the church. By his encouragement a Youth Club was eventually started following successful social evenings. The 30 – 35 youngsters who made up the membership of the club came from the uniformed organisations of Roscoe. One or two lay helpers also gave their time to help make this venture worthwhile. In this way Malcolm Furness was released to attend to matters of concern in the wider community served by Roscoe Place.

One of these 'was the fact that many children were left to look after themselves on leaving school in the afternoon and in school holidays'. Malcolm Furness says: 'All-the-year-round children's work began in **Chapeltown in 1967** when a group of interested local people (***Dr Julia Fourman, Diana Phillip** and others*) established a steering committee which eventually became the Studley Grange Children's Association'. They opened the **Studley Grange Play Centre** at 55 Louis Street. That centre provided activities for 3 -5 year olds during the day, 5 – 8 year olds after school hours and a Girls' Club for 8 – 14 year on Thursday and Saturday afternoons. Malcolm Furness played an effective part in helping to bring this Centre into being.

With an extra member of staff, and the help of volunteers, Roscoe Place was able to organise a **Play Scheme** (one of three in the circuit that year) during the summer **school holidays of 1967**—a venture which continued for some years. That summer they were assisted by two young American students (*Winant Volunteers from the USA)* who brought their own exuberance to this project. The Leaders' Meeting Minutes of November 1967 report Malcolm as saying that "1390 children had attended the Holiday Place Scheme (over five weeks), an average of 65 per day with outdoor and indoor activities. The Director of Education had also expressed his appreciation of the work done and they would consider helping on a future occasion". Malcolm Furness comments *(See his* Reminiscences *in Appendix)*

> "The Winant Volunteers helped us to run the first large-scale Holiday Play Scheme in Leeds – probably the first in the country. On the first morning we had a queue of boys and girls waiting at 8.30am, and we ran all the month of August ... a pattern for what later became national holiday schemes. That was a great success, and one of which Roscoe can be justly proud."

Another significant venture which started in 1967 were the **monthly Working Lunches** for social workers from the Education, Social Welfare and Probation departments of local government, along with interested local doctors and police who met at Roscoe with Miss Mary Stratton being the Hostess/Chairman. These lunches lasted for about a decade, from the days of Malcolm Furness to those of Trevor Bates.

In **September 1967** the **Revd Kenneth Glendinning** replaced Gerald Bostock as a probationer in the circuit, working alongside Malcolm. Ken brought his own distinctive personality and style of approach which proved to be so appropriate for that section of the circuit. Ken took up the task of continuing the work among young people and the Youth Club started by Gerald Bostock. A coffee bar was built, a magazine produced and collecting for Christian Aid took place as well as the re-decoration of a vestry to be used as a lounge. A Sponsored Walk for "Project 150" South India was organised and the Club won three Cups in Circuit Sports Competitions. Up to 100 youngsters were involved in the Club that year.

In **September 1968** Ken was moved from that section of the circuit and was given responsibility for Trinity and Ashley Road churches. The **Revd Peter Williamson** replaced him as probationer colleague with Malcolm Furness and remained until August 1971, when he was transferred to be minister for Ashley Road and Cambridge, Meanwood Road churches. Peter encouraged the formation of a Youth Choir and of a Drama Group to enable youngsters to participate in Passion Week services and other occasions. Suffice to say that a great deal of positive work was done in the Roscoe Place Youth Club with youngsters on a

Thursday evening during the time of all three probationers, and this stood Roscoe Methodist Church in very good stead for the future.

However, during the 1960s the Roscoe Place building and site were in jeopardy because it was surrounded by housing demolition in neighbouring streets and the Roscoe buildings were being badly vandalised.

ON THE MOVE: WHEN AND WHERE?

In **November 1965** Malcolm Furness reported to the Roscoe Place **Leaders' Meeting** that the Leeds Corporation had indicated they might require the Church premises in connection with Town Planning schemes in 3 – 5 years time. The Corporation were willing to enter into negotiations in 1966 about an alternative site.

At the **Leaders Meeting** of **February 1967** Malcolm Furness reported on discussions within the circuit:

> "about the possible future of Roscoe, Trinity and Ashley Road churches. It was not clear where a new church should be sited until there was more information from the Town Planning Department. Possibly two churches instead of three, or even one united church on a large scale". A joint Leaders' Meeting of the three churches was arranged in April for discussion about the matter, and at the May Leaders' Meeting for Roscoe it was reported that: "it was agreed that a single new Church should eventually replace the three existing Societies (congregations)".

At the **August 1967 Leaders' Meeting** Malcolm Furness reported:

> "a rumour had reached him that, due to a change in the Civic Development Plan, St. Clements' *(Anglican)* and Roscoe Churches would no longer be required by the Corporation. The rumour was reported to the Superintendent Minister who discovered from the City Engineer that a change of plan had been approved ... the final plan now agreed would leave St. Clements' buildings unaffected, but the position of Roscoe

remained unchanged. Roscoe buildings would be required by the Corporation....but not until **1972 or 1973**. The Chairman (Malcolm Furness) indicated that this postponement made it more urgently necessary to persuade the Corporation to anticipate the compulsory purchase of our premises, so that we might proceed with rebuilding plans ..."

The **Trustees' Meeting of October 1969** was informed by the Revd W. Stainer-Smith:

"that negotiations had been proceeding with Leeds Corporation whose final decision was still awaited. However, the situation seemed bleak because of the financial difficulties and the high cost of borrowing by the Corporation for re-development projects. Two alternatives seemed possible and were minuted ... Mr Harry Cocksedge urged an early decision must be obtained – do   we go or do we stay? The state of uncertainty over the last   3 or 4 years was detrimental to all that was being done."

In **August 1970** Malcolm Furness moved to an appointment in Morecambe one year earlier than was originally planned. In September the **Revd Michael Chapman** was stationed in the circuit as the minister for Roscoe Place.

At the **February 18th 1971 Trustees Meeting:** "Mr David Bradshaw (*Estate Agent*) was introduced. He indicated that Leeds Corporation were willing to make a compromise settlement" and "to pay up to £55,000 for Roscoe Place premises or such smaller (amount) as is used for re-instatement purposes". "Alternative sites were available or likely." "This is a verbal offer and nothing had been put in writing at this stage".

At the **February 25th 1971 Leaders' Meeting** the Minutes state that:

"Mr Chapman explained that the Corporation were now offering to look into the question of a new site. The Trustees and Sub-Building Committee are now negotiating and members of the Building Committee are meeting various architects and

63

visiting a few comparatively new churches, to try and decide which type would be the most suitable for our requirements. Mr Chapman had also drawn up a Plan, showing the type of building he had in mind and Mr Bradshaw was submitting this to the Corporation with a view to being offered a suitable site."

The **April 1971 Trustees' Meeting** recommended that the architects for the new Roscoe Church be Messrs John Brunton & Partners of Bradford.

The **June 1971 Leaders' Meeting** was informed that: "an architect had been appointed and had met with the Building Committee, and was drawing up a Plan of a suitable new building". The **September Leaders' Meeting** was told that: "the City Planning Committee was holding us up, as they still will not say when we can have a new site in spite of being pressed for such a decision by the Superintendent Minister (*Revd W. Stainer-Smith*) and Mr Chapman, etc."

At the **Trustees' Meeting in March 1972 new trustees** were appointed. (*See Appendix*) To eleven long standing members were added **Jessie Peacock, John Connor, Myrna Anita Tyrell, James Arthur Saddler, Sarah Lunn, Lily Atkinson, Ethel Sedman, Charles William Burgess, Charles Eric Griffiths and Allan Joseph Herbert**. The latter had previously been appointed Chapel Steward in Mr Harrison's place at the Trustees' Meeting of August 1970.

The Trustees were also informed that "Mr David Bradshaw and J. Brunton & Partners had protracted negotiations with Leeds Corporation – and a building site for the new Church was offered at the corner of Chapeltown Road and Francis Street."

The **May 1972 Leaders' Meeting** heard that "**Revd Trevor Bates** would commence his ministry at Roscoe at the beginning of December and it was possible we would have the help of a probationer. In the interim period the Revd K. Glendinning would be in charge at Roscoe" together with a new probationer, **Revd Ian G. Lucraft**. Regarding the proposed new building, the meeting was told that:

"The Architect had drawn up Plans according to our specification but this would now cost much more than the amount to be given by the Corporation and even with the £7000 granted from Lincoln Field Trust, this would not cover the cost. Application had been made to the Corporation for a higher amount owing to the delay in their giving us a site. The result was that the District Surveyor and Valuer had spent some time looking around our buildings and had stated the matter was being treated as "Urgent"."

At the **October 1972 Trustees' Meeting the Revd Ian Lucraft** suggested:

"the Citizen's Advice Bureau (CAB) might be interested in the use of room at the new premises, and if so, this would help with maintenance and running costs and it might be advantageous to add additional room for this purpose, especially if the **Vic Hallam** scheme were adopted. This matter would receive attention."

The **May 1973 Trustees' Meeting** was informed that "Tenders had been received from five bidders:

J.J. Ewbank & Co. Ltd.	£70,128.14
W.T. Abbots Ltd.	£67,471.20
Leonard Smith	£66,940.00
Roy Parkinson	£70,125.60
R.R. Roberts	£67,770.00

Seating to be 176 inclusive of additional side chairs. A variation to the scheme regarding the separation of the Sunday School room from the Main Hall, with an elevation of 2'6"; giving further space for 50 seats. To include Car Park and Landscaping, organ, chairs, tables, kitchen equipment, cooker and crockery etc. Carpets in Lounge and Vestry, plus Professional Fees = £87,000 total.

"For the CAB two offices to be incorporated in the new building, to be rented. This is agreed by CAB and letter has

65

been received from them dealing with terms of agreement and a weekly payment of £4 to be reviewed. CAB responsible for internal decoration."

"The meeting agreed in principle. Matter to be remitted to Chapel Department in Manchester. Two Year agreement to be renewed after that period".

The **May 1973 Leaders' Meeting** was informed that:

"Detailed Plans had been approved and a Tender accepted at £86,000 and after the District Valuer had received this we hoped the building would be started about July". However, it wasn't until **February 1974** that the **Leaders Meeting** could be informed that: the "**Stonelaying would be on 6th April.**"

The lack of "urgency" which seemed apparent in trying to finalise an agreement between the Leeds Corporation and the Roscoe Place Trustees came to a head in the **summer of 1973**. A couple of coincidences occurred:

First there was a crisis in the community about Cowper Street School. At a Public Meeting of the Chapeltown Parents' Action Group on Sunday **June 24th Mrs Louise Crumbie** was a spokesperson who outlined the changes they urged the Department of Education to do something about. On Monday **June 25th** the parents of children at that school went on strike. 'Virtually no black children attended the school and parents demonstrated outside the school for action to be taken to change things.' This protest and demonstration brought to a head a number of dissatisfactions felt in the community of Chapeltown about the Leeds Corporation's lack of understanding and willingness to improve conditions for West Indian people and their families.

The second coincidence was a chance meeting that summer which Trevor Bates had with **Councillor Wm. (Bill) Merritt** who had been Deputy Mayor of Leeds in **1972/1973**, and was a former boy in the **13th Leeds Boys' Brigade Company**. Bill Merritt was also one of the longest serving councillors on the City Council at that time. Bill promised to intercede on our behalf with the Corporation to try and

66

bring about a final settlement for the Roscoe Place Methodist Church re-instatement. Within days the Leeds Corporation agreed to pay up to half the valuation of the Roscoe Place premises, valued at £264,000, so agreeing to meet costs of a new site and the building of a new church up to the value of £132,000.

The **September 1973 Trustees' Meeting** was informed by the Revd Stainer Smith that "we could expect to receive a cheque from Leeds Corporation for the sum of £88,400. ...The contract had gone to Leonard Smith, the lowest of five bidders, for £66,940."

However, at the **December 1973 Trustees'** Meeting **Leonard Smith** submitted a revised tender for £76,302 due to the national emergency, with extra costs for the site of £10,000 and a further £1,000 for landscaping. A Letter of Intent was to be sent to **Vic Hallam** with instructions to Leonard Smith and the contract to be signed later. The total cost of the building would be approximately £100,000.

The architects were instructed to proceed. Mr Philip Senior and/or Mr John Goddard became the on-site visiting architects throughout the construction period. The **corner site of Francis Street and Chapeltown Road** was purchased from Leeds City Corporation and the new Church to be built there. This was the site of Willow House, which had been the home of the Benjamin Randall Vickers family, and the re-instatement proved to be a providential and historic venture.

REMINISCENCES FOUR

MY CHURCH, ROSCOE METHODIST

THE FIRST TIME I worshipped at Roscoe Place Methodist Church, was in November 1959, after arriving from St Kitts. There were about 50 worshippers present at the Sunday morning service. This was conducted by Revd Russell Moston, in a similar pattern to the services in the Methodist Churches in St Kitts. Most of the hymns were written by Charles Wesley and were well known to me. I was warmly welcomed by the minister and other members.

In July 1968, I was married at Roscoe Place by the Revd Kenneth Glendinning, following which I lived abroad for several years.

On my return to Chapeltown permanently, I became involved in the life of the present Roscoe. I am now the Senior Church Steward. Roscoe will always be my Church.

Myrtle Oke

I WAS BORN on May 25th 2005 and I was christened at Roscoe Methodist Church. I have attended Sunday School almost every Sunday with my grandma and I love it!

Adetoro Adeleke-Oke
(Granddaughter of Myrtle)

THE CHURCH IN MY LIFE AND WITNESS FOR CHRIST

I CAME from the island of St Kitts in the Caribbean to England in 1959, age 23. As a practising Christian, the Church has always meant a great deal to me. I nurtured a great sense of belonging. I didn't hesitate to enter into that great fellowship of God's people in Leeds.

68

STRANGE

I felt strange among the people obviously, but I also felt a part of the mystery of the worship, and that was some measure of the continuity of that something in me from back home. My denomination at that time was Church of England. However, I was very happy to worship at Roscoe Place Chapel, Chapeltown Road near Sheepscar, after marrying a Methodist local preacher (Arthur) from the island of Nevis, who was already a member. Many more West Indians made their spiritual home at Roscoe, and I soon found fellowship and friendship within the church. There was a very strong and influential white membership, and their loyalty and love for the church was evident. We were invited into the homes of some of the white members, close ties and respect developed and still remains today.

ACITIVITIES

The Anglo West Indian Fellowship was held in the Roscoe Hall following every Sunday evening service. White and black members participated. Favourite hymns and a prayer meeting followed informally, and I loved it very much and felt revived. My spiritual and social life was enhanced by the church through the Choir, Sunday School, and the role of Class Leader. My faith deepened as a now much smaller congregation prayed for the new Roscoe Methodist Church which was going to be built where the church originally started further up Chapeltown Road. This was completed in 1974.

WITNESS FOR CHRIST

In witnessing for Christ I could not do without him. The great Methodist Covenant Service which is held on every first Sunday in January, takes hold of me every time I hear it. It empties me and it refills me. These words speak to me – 'Christ has many services to be done, some are easy, others are difficult, some bring honour, others bring reproach, some are suitable to our natural inclinations and material interests, others are contrary to both.' Based at Roscoe the West Indian Family Counselling Service is the practical witness and outreach to our community in Christ's name. For some years I have worked for WIFCOS, and cherish the fulfilment of a humble servant for Christ. Personally speaking, the church is Christ in His followers, yesterday, today and forever.

Mary Saddler 1984

JOURNEYING WITH ROSCOE ALL THE WAY

I HOLD MOST DEARLY many memories of both my spiritual and vocational journey with Roscoe all of the way within the former and present churches. It was my late husband, Arthur Saddler, who introduced me to Roscoe Place Methodist Church. After attending for some time, I was invited to join the choir and also the Sunday School. I love to sing and was delighted to be asked as it gave me the feeling that I belonged more fully to the church family and was contributing to the worship. In those days Sunday School was held in the afternoon at 2.30pm and the attendance was over one hundred. I was asked to help with the Junior section and became committed to the children's ministry and I'm still presently involved.

I enjoyed various coach trips and outings which were organised by the late Mr Roland Lunn. For example we went to the seaside, the Lake District, visited Gretna Green and other places like Coventry Cathedral. The fun we had has remained in my memory. A church holiday at Cliff College for one week is another memorable experience.

My integration into the ministry of both churches was unsophisticated. I was able to build on the early experiences gained through my involvement with the activities which existed. I then moved on to paid work as the second WIFCOS Worker and developed the Roscoe Luncheon Club for the Elderly during the duration of my employment with the project.

That period spanned twenty one years which has been a vocation that has enriched my life immensely. I value the support and respect that many people including all of the ministers who have chaired the WIFCOS Project gave me over the years and for which I am deeply grateful.

Mary Saddler 2010

ROSCOE METHODIST CHUIRCH

I FIRST ATTENDED Roscoe Place Methodist Church in 1959. At that time I had no idea that it was the church that most black immigrants attended. I noticed this church whilst I was on my journey on the bus to and from town (Leeds). Then I understood that the minister there was very kind to West Indians, helping them to find lodgings and settle them down in Leeds.

I found that there was a warm welcome at the church, which made people always want to attend church. I recall telling one of my work mates that I attended Roscoe Place Methodist Church. She said that her family attended that church in her youth but did not attend church any more. She assured me that Roscoe was a nice church and that they got many bowls of hot soup there during the war. The soup she said, kept many poor children from the area alive. It was then I realised that Roscoe was a historical and respected church.

It was there that the first Wesley Guild started. It had the first all black Girls' Brigade and Boys' Brigade Companies in Leeds and maybe in England. It once had a very thriving youth club that was run by the Deaconesses and Probationer ministers. The youth club was vital for it kept our children off the streets. The church also sent its first black youth to Switzerland to represent the Leeds North East circuit and British Methodism at the European Methodist Youth Conference in 1978. The youth was my son, Ray Tyrell, and he was very proud of himself for being able to do it. He said that it was an experience he's not likely to forget.

Roscoe Place Methodist Church was a large and draughty building. It was cold at times during the winter; you needed gloves on during the sermon. As the building got colder and the needs of the people in the area changed, the younger generation became more affluent and there was no more need for the bowls of soup, The church building suffered with broken windows caused by stone throwing. The upkeep of the building became an impossible task, so it was demolished and the new Roscoe Methodist Church was built in 1974, on the spot where the Roscoe Place Methodist Church was started by the Vickers family. I am glad to have played an active part in this famous church called Roscoe.

71

Roscoe must be the only church in the world that has influenced four young black boys into music and helped to encourage them financially and physically. One of them, Andrew Saddler, is now our organist. Another, Mervyn Williams, has taken up music as his profession and listening to him playing the organ at York Minster brought tears to the eyes of those of us who were present. One other, Collin Robinson, on joining the RAF played in an RAF Band in Cyprus. The other event at York Minster that brought tears to my eyes was hearing the members of Roscoe Girls' and Boys' Brigades playing, 'O Lord My God When I In Awesome Wonder', which was played on the Steel Band Pans. It was really inspiring.

We have had very good ministers who believed in us without prejudice and pushed us on, but none more so than the Reverend Trevor Bates. That is in my view, for I don't know about the other members' views.

I am sure there are many more memorable happenings that occurred and still are occurring at Roscoe.

Myrna Tyrell

GOD IS GOOD

IN 1966 I CAME TO LIVE in Chapeltown, Leeds. After a while I started to attend Roscoe Place Methodist Church. My three children were christened here.

After Roscoe Place Church building was demolished due to the new road system, I continued to attend the services in the new and present building, in the evening. Later I attended the morning services, where I met a few people who later became good friends. I felt "at home" in Roscoe and enjoyed most the services.

When the Saturday School started, at the request of the minister, I was one of the volunteers. We had to settle the children until the students from the college came to assist them with their reading and maths. After the lesson refreshments were served.

Shortly after, I was asked by Mary Saddler to help her start the Roscoe Luncheon Club, with other church members. At first I was a volunteer working one day a week, then two days a week. Later I became a paid employee. We worked very hard to keep the Club running. Its members were from all the churches in the community. I made lots of friends and worked here until my retirement. I am again a volunteer.

I support all the projects at Roscoe, such as the Women's Fellowship, and enjoy attending Roscoe Services every Sunday.

GOD IS GOOD AND TO GOD BE THE GLORY.

Joyce Vernon (1934-2011)

Roscoe Place Sunday School Primary Department about 1965

73

Chapter Five

SERVING THE WIDER COMMUNITY / A PROMISING FUTURE
1972 – 1981

When the **Revd Trevor Bates** arrived in the Leeds North East circuit on 1st December 1972 to work with Roscoe Place, two things were uppermost on the Church's agenda. First, to try and find ways of persuading Leeds Corporation to finalise their verbal agreement to purchase Roscoe Place Church premises for an acceptable amount in order to secure a new site and build a new church. In Chapter Three we explained how this happened in the summer of 1973. Secondly anticipating the official closing of Roscoe Place and a new Church being built, efforts to raise additional money had to be organised. Applications for grants and appeals for financial help were made to ensure that the re-instatement could be completed free of debt.

One major money raising effort took place on Friday evening 28th September 1973. A **Caribbean Artists Concert** was staged at Roscoe Place Church when four professional Caribbean artists journeyed from London and graciously gave of their talents and time. They were Nadia Cattouse, singer (ex Belize), Frankie Reneau, pianist/organist, composer (ex Belize), Winston Colbourne, singer/entertainer with Pontin's Holiday Centres (ex Jamaica) and Jamal Ali, rapper artist (ex Jamaica). We managed to attract a lot of local support, making it a memorable evening. We hoped this event would signal to the community some of the capabilities and artistic achievements of black people!

THE NEW ROSCOE METHODIST CHURCH

The **Dedication of Site and Bricklaying** for the new Roscoe Methodist Church took place on **Saturday April 6th 1974** at the corner site of Chapeltown Road and Francis Street. Among those who took part were the Leeds North East Circuit Superintendent Minister, the **Revd W. Stainer-Smith**, the Revd Trevor S. Bates and probationer the Revd Ian G. Lucraft, along with the architect, Mr John Goddard. Symbolically, bricks were laid by several lay members of the congregation representing old and young. The event was followed by a tea arranged at Roscoe Place Methodist Church.

Bricklaying Ceremony for the new church, April 1974. The Revd W. Stainer Smith, Superintendent Minister; Mr John Goddard, architect; Miss Ethel Sedman of the congregation

The **Thanksgiving Service and Final Act of Worship at Roscoe Place Methodist Church**, Sheepscar, took place on Sunday **29th September 1974** at 3pm. The service was conducted by Trevor Bates assisted by probationer Revd Raymond Garfoot. Mr T.B. Simpson and Miss Joyce Reyner read scripture lessons and the sermon was preached by **Revd W. Stainer-Smith**.

The **new Roscoe Methodist Church was officially opened on Saturday October 5th 1974** at 3pm. Those present were The Lord Mayor of Leeds Cllr. Jean de Carteret, Chairman of the Leeds District Revd Walker Lee, the Superintendent Minister the Revd W. Stainer-Smith, the minister in Pastoral Charge, the Revd Trevor S. Bates, the visiting preacher the Revd J. Malcolm Furness, together with other

75

circuit ministers. Bible readings were read by a church steward and children of the Sunday School. The preacher at the evening service at 7.30pm was the Revd Harry Salmon. The final cost of the new facilities was £110,000, but it took another three years to clear the outstanding debt of £3,000. The situation was partly eased by raising a loan of £1500 from the Leeds District Extension Fund.

To mark the opening of the new Church a plaque was secured to the right hand wall in the Entrance Hall. It reads as follows:

**To the Glory of God
Father Son and Holy Spirit
and for service to all people in the community
this building was opened on 5th October 1974.
This plaque also Records with Thankfulness the
Work, Worship And Witness of the Methodist Congregation begun
in 1849 on this Site in the Preaching Room of Willow House
belonging to Mr Benjamin Randall Vickers and continued at
Roscoe Place Chapel 1862-1974**

ORGANISTS

Mr **Leslie Farnill** had been organist from 1925 to 1973, choirmaster for many of those years and editor of the Roscoe Place Newsletter since 1964. Malcolm Furness pays tribute to him separately (*see Appendix*). Mr Farnill was outstanding in his devotion, the quality of his playing and his dedicated leadership for the Roscoe Place congregation. In his latter year or two Leslie invited a friend, **Mr George Stoker,** to assist with playing the organ at Roscoe Place, but it became clear that neither Leslie nor George would be able to continue playing for any length of time because of their increasing ages!

The new church had a pipe organ, built and installed by Laycock and Bannister Organ Builders of Crosshills, near Skipton, at the special request of the West Indian members of Roscoe. The official Dedication of the Organ took place within a Concert Evening held at Roscoe on Saturday 18th January 1975. The Chairperson was Mr A. Eric Holland,

76

the **Guest Organist** was **Mr David Wilks** of Lidgett Park Methodist Church, and the **Chapel Allerton Methodist Church Choir**, under the leadership of **Mr David Carr**, took part in the evening's programme.

Roscoe now faced the difficult task of trying to recruit people to play this organ on a regular basis! George Stoker continued to play for a time, together with **Cliff Haresign** (*a friend of Ian Lucraft*) and **Elaine Turner** (*a helper with the Youth Club*); however, this arrangement could not last. Something else needed to be done. We suddenly realised that three teenage boys, belonging to West Indian families in the congregation, could play the piano in some measure. They were **Andrew Saddler, Colin Robinson and Stephen Woodley**. George Stoker offered to tutor them at his own home to play the hymns for the worship services at Roscoe. The preachers appointed for Roscoe's Sunday services were requested to provide their hymn numbers ten days in advance – what an opportunity and what a challenge! Very soon a fourth youngster was included in the team, namely **Mervyn Williams,** a neighbour and friend of Colin Robinson. This proved to be the beginning of a very special chapter in the life of Roscoe. In October 1975, because George Stoker was not well enough to continue being an organist, Roscoe expressed their appreciation and bade him farewell. However, George did continue to support our teenage organists with tuition at his home for some time.

For a couple of years Roscoe encouraged four budding organists to attend the **"Youth Makes Music"** weekends held annually (*first at Kesteven College, near Grantham, Lincolnshire and then at Birmingham*), organised by the Methodist Church Youth Dept. Because the four youngsters showed such promise special grants were offered by the **Freeman Trust of the Methodist Church Music Society** to meet most of the tuition fees for the teenage organists for two years. This ensured that Roscoe's Sunday worship services would have a team of four organists available on a rota from our own congregation! Little did we know then that 25 years hence **Mervyn** would be an accomplished organist and teacher of music, with a distinguished career, who in the summer of 2000 was guest organist along with Bath University College Choir at York Minster for one week!

Four young organists, all of Roscoe families, about 1978: left to right:
Stephen Woodley, Colin Robinson, Mervyn Williams and Andrew Saddler

FIRST OCCASIONS AT THE NEW ROSCOE:

The first wedding to take place in the new Roscoe Methodist Church was that between Miss Gloria Simmonds and Mr Hughbon Condor on Saturday 12th October 1974, conducted by Trevor Bates. Jason Pennycooke is proud to claim that he was the first baby baptised there.

On Sunday March 27th 1977 (*Passion Sunday*) Granada TV televised the morning service live. The service was led by Trevor Bates with Revd Howard O. Smith and Sister Margaret E. Horn with members of the congregations taking part. The organist was Mervyn Williams, 13 years old! The theme for the service was: 'The Church as Servant – of the past, of the present, and of the future'.

PASTORAL LEADERSHIP

The transitional process to achieve **Church leadership** which was more representative of the congregation continued with the appointment of several new **Class Leaders and Assistants** at the Leaders' Meeting in Autumn 1973. The revised list of five white English and 14 West Indian leaders was:

Elsie Ackroyd	Cedric Clark
Enid Claxton	John Connor
Louise Crumbie	Wilhelmina Delaney
Eileen Elliott	Elsie Farrar
Roland Lunn	Sarah Lunn
Dorothy Lunn	Morley Molyneaux
Myrtle Oke	Elsie Plumb
Arthur Saddler	Mary Saddler
Leonora Thompson	Myrna Tyrell
Georgina Webbe	

This coincided with the Leaders' Meeting agreeing to Roscoe's Membership Roll being divided up into residential zones to make it easier for Class Leaders to maintain pastoral contact with their Class Members.

MEMBERSHIP OVERVIEW

The Church Membership figures across the years offer a changing picture of belonging, particularly as the transition began to take place from an all-white English congregation in 1915 to a predominantly West Indian congregation in 1981. The figures we have been able to obtain are as follow:

September 1915	217	May 1967	120
November 1917	213	February 1969	129
March 1923	216	November 1970	115
December 1923	144	May 1973	114
January 1938	158	February 1974	135
November 1963	124	February 1975	151
November 1964	129	October 1980	177
August 1965	127	October 1981	166
November 1966	122		

79

We have previously noted the big drop in membership in 1923 and speculated whether this was due to the anticipated union of the three Methodist denominations which took place in 1932, or the post-WWI doubts about church commitment? The second noticeable trend is that once West Indians started belonging to Roscoe the membership fluctuated until the new Roscoe Church building was opened and then there was a substantial rise during the 1970s reaching a peak of 177 in 1980. The Circuit *(Financial)* Assessment was based on 170 from September 1981.

MORE LAY OFFICERS

The September 1973 Leaders' Meeting agreed to combine the **Society and Trust Accounts** "as from that month in order to reduce Bank charges, if the Trustees agreed". This heralded the necessity to combine the Trust and Society Accounts required after the Methodist Church Act 1976 when the responsibilities of Trust and Society would be combined within a Church Council. **Harry Cocksedge** was the Trust Accounts Treasurer with **Ernest Poulter** as the Society Accounts Treasurer. At the December 1973 Leaders' Meeting both treasurers indicated they wished to resign. It was then suggested that an approach be made to **Mr Okoro Ndukwe**, a Nigerian member who had worshipped with us for a year or two whilst studying at Leeds University and who was now qualified in Accountancy. This was done and he was appointed the new **Church Treasurer** responsible for both sets of accounts as from January 1974.

Okuro and Oyidiya Ndukwe were married at Roscoe Place on 10th March 1973 by the Revd Ian G. Lucraft and they remained committed to Roscoe. Okuro also, prior to going to Nepal, volunteered to be Treasurer for the **Chapeltown Adventure Playground.** In the following years they had three children and January 1981, because Okuro was accepted for service overseas by the Methodist Church Overseas Division, they all flew from Yeadon Airport to Kathmandu to live and serve in **Nepal** for five years.

At the March 1976 Church Council meeting **Lay Chairmen** for four of the main Church Committees were recommended for the first time to the Circuit Meeting for ratification. They were: **Church Family**: Mr Arthur Saddler; **Neighbourhood**: Mr John Connor; **World Service & Mission**: Mr Cedric Clarke and **Finance**: Mr Roland Lunn. This was another new step taken towards greater self-management for Roscoe Church, providing a larger lay team.

CITIZENS ADVICE BUREAU FOR CHAPELTOWN

At Ian Lucraft's suggestion to the Trustees' Meeting of October 1972 provision was made in the new Church to accommodate the Chapeltown Citizens Advice Bureau. The CAB started in 1972 and was housed provisionally in the first Sikh Ramgharia building on Chapeltown Road. After the opening of new Roscoe in October 1974 the CAB moved into two rooms by prior arrangement and rental agreement and **Mrs Jennie Macklay** was their Organiser. The rent for the first year was £300. The Chapeltown CAB Annual Reports reflect how in the early years of its life this CAB handled increasing numbers of enquiries on a whole range of problems, so that the team of workers needed to be increased from year to year – both funded and volunteers. In 1972/73 1343 enquiries were dealt with but in 1976/77 the numbers had risen to 6858! The demand for more and more rooms to accommodate additional office space and interviewing rooms became incessant. From 1972/73 to 1979/80 the annual number of enquiries dealt with increased tenfold to 13,879!

Because of the multi-ethnic and multi-cultural nature of the Chapeltown and Harehills communities it was recognised that Chapeltown CAB was becoming one of the most skilled and experienced branches of Citizens Advice Bureaux in the UK. We are not surprised therefore that the importance and growth of the Chapeltown Citizens Advice Bureau became one of the early warning signs that Roscoe Methodist Church may need to consider extending their premises in the near future if only to adequately house the CAB if Roscoe wished to retain them as tenants!

ROSCOE DAY NURSERY

The second venture housed at Roscoe Methodist Church was a new **Day Nursery**. This was the brain-child of **Mrs Oma Notay** an East African immigrant with Indian family origins who was of the Hindu faith, who approached Roscoe with a view to using our premises. By agreement the Roscoe Day Nursery was opened in September 1976, but only the large Fellowship Room could be made available for that purpose. The Church Council was informed in March 1977 that "the Day Nursery was developing rapidly and is still progressing. There are 12 – 14 children attending".

The Annual Church Meeting of February 1978 was told that "55 children had been cared for during 1977, and 17 were cared for on a daily basis". By 1979 **Miss Georgina Webbe** became an additional member of the nursery team.

This Nursery was well used and for many years cared for the maximum number of children permitted by the authorities i.e. 20. The Nursery was recognised by the local authority for its service to the community and was given grant-aid for one full-time and one part-time member of staff. This was yet another reason for Roscoe to consider extending the premises, to provide more adequate facilities for the Nursery staff and children.

Miss Georgina Webbe, April 1974.
(Dorothy Bates and a Trinity member
in the background)

WEST INDIAN FAMILY COUNSELLING SERVICE

During 1978 it became evident to members of Roscoe's congregation that the domestic problems occurring with local West Indian families warranted special concern and pastoral help. Conversations with Trevor Bates and Sister Margaret Horn prompted exploring the possibilities of starting a West Indian Family Counselling Service which hopefully would offer help to the West Indian community throughout Leeds. The Annual Church Meeting of February 1979 was informed of this as a new venture, and the Church Council of March 1979 confirmed the decision to appoint a West Indian Family Counsellor. The WIFCOS was funded by monies from the Rowntree Charitable Trust (£2500) and the Methodist Church Social Responsibility Committee's **Fund for Multi-Racial Projects** (£1000) for a minimum three-year project. The post would be advertised in *The Methodist Recorder* and interviewing done by a panel to include the minister and members of Roscoe's Neighbourhood Committee.

Whilst it seemed urgent to launch this new venture in September 1979, trying to find sufficient office space at Roscoe for a Counsellor at this time of congested use of our premises was a real challenge! Eventually it was agreed that the Choir Vestry should be made available for this purpose. The first WIFCOS worker appointed was **Mr S. Emmanuel Kebbe,** a West African émigré from Sierra Leone who impressed us with his enthusiasm to tackle this new venture. It was agreed that there would be a six months probationary period (until February 1980), and then, given satisfaction of both sides, a contract for three years would be drawn up. However, it was necessary to terminate Mr Kebbie's employment due to gross misconduct on October 14th 1980. For eight months WIFCOS had to be suspended until a new worker could take up the task.

Of real help at that time were **Richard and Kate Pinder**, a Methodist couple who had recently returned from working in Zambia, and were living in the area, who showed an interest in Roscoe's life and work. Kate volunteered some time as an assistant to the counsellor and Richard joined the Management Committee. **Mrs Mary Saddler**, a member of Roscoe and a resident of Chapeltown, was selected from several applicants and appointed in June 1981 and was given the freedom to develop her own style of counselling and new purpose for this endeavour by Roscoe. There is no doubt that Richard Pinder's help and guidance were crucial in this transition period.

CHANGE IN EMPHASIS FOR WEEKLY ACTIVITIES

It appears that the gradual change in the nature of the congregation at Roscoe Place was being reflected in the kind of activities which took place on a weekly basis. Throughout the 1960s the uniformed organisations— i.e. Boys' Brigade, Life Boys, Girl Guides and Brownies—were having difficulty in securing enough leadership to maintain their work among children and young people. West Indian youngsters were attending these groups, but the future of the groups seemed uncertain. When **Joyce Reyner** became **Guide Commissioner for Leeds, Mrs Walter Hall** took on the Guide Company Captaincy, but it was a struggle. The Brownies folded in July 1971 because parents were reluctant to let their girls come to Roscoe in the evenings. The Boys' Brigade Captaincy and Life Boy Leadership changed hands several times and the Company eventually folded in 1969.

At the same time Youth Club work and Play Centre activities seemed to be more attractive with the special attention and encouragement given by the probationer ministers who worked with them. There is no doubt that the youth work was still very difficult because there was a limited number of lay helpers from the congregation, not enough to cope with the numbers of youngsters attending. Whenever the congregation moved into new Church premises it was evident that a new start would be necessary working with children and young people.

Sunday School, Youth Club and Holiday Play Projects got under way relatively easily from October 1974 in the new Roscoe. The enthusiasm of Ian Lucraft, who was able to recruit additional helpers, enabled a new Youth Club to be started with up to 120 teenagers. The Sunday School, staffed by members of the congregation, also quickly got into its stride, especially with the younger age groups. In the summer of 1975 a successful Play Project was held for several weeks, and at one point became an embarrassment because of the number of youngsters attending!

A new undertaking for Roscoe, rather than re-starting Girl Guides and Brownies, was the launch of a **Girls' Brigade Company,** and to do so with leadership from within the congregation. The formation of the **27th Leeds Girls' Brigade Company** was started in 1975 with **Miss Elsie Plumb** as Captain and a team of officers: Mary Saddler, Georgina Webbe, Dorothy Lunn, Louise Crumbie and Myrna Tyrell and Trevor Bates as Chaplain. Myrna Tyrell eventually took over from Elsie Plumb and possibly was the first black G.B. Captain in Leeds. Very quickly the GB Company had forty girls in uniform. The next big step was the venture to re-start the **13th Leeds Boys' Brigade Company** with **Mr L. George Eubanks** as Captain, nine additional officers and helpers from the congregation with Trevor Bates as Chaplain. The Company started on 9th October, and the Life Boys section in December 1977, whilst the official enrolment for both took place on 19th February 1978. In 1981 **Mr Allan Herbert** took over as Company Captain (later that year **Revd John Whittle** took over the Chaplaincy) holding the Company together until 1985 when it finally ceased to meet.

Mrs Sarah Lunn with a Sunday School class in the 1990s

GOOD HOUSE-KEEPING

Over the years the congregations in both buildings have found themselves being challenged to meet the financial commitments of not only maintaining their premises, but also meeting their commitments to the circuit as churches staffed by ministers with particular gifts for our situation. In later years the new Roscoe premises offered the possibility of renting space and facilities to community groups which would also help with maintenance costs. However, there was an endemic financial challenge which needed to be addressed.

In 1955 The Leaders' Meeting was informed that the giving averaged £8 per week which needed to be supplemented with monies from special efforts and festivals in order to meet Roscoe's annual commitments. In 1964 a Christian Stewardship Programme was carried out which improved the practice of visiting by Pastoral Visitors and brought about more generous giving by the congregation. The Weekly

86

Envelope pledges system has had a chequered life since the Trustees of Roscoe Place commended this way of disciplined giving as far back as 1921! Some members were very loyal, whilst others faltered. The Leaders' Meeting of August 1970 was informed that the weekly giving in collections was £22.7s 7d in loose cash plus £17.8s.0d from pledged giving, but was failing to meet their commitments.

Once the congregation moved into the new Roscoe building the whole question of finance needed to be reviewed. Apart from meeting the final expenditure on the new premises the congregation were made aware of the fact that for several years they had been receiving a Home Mission grant of £250 per year. Trevor Bates wrote in the April 1974 issue of the Newsletter:

"Now that we are at the point of having a new suite of premises for our work and people, there can be no reason for not wanting to bear our part of the financial   obligation   of running the circuit, and paying more towards the ministry of our own congregation and area."

"At the moment our Circuit Assessment for Roscoe is frozen at £640 per year, and has been for many years. Because of the big increase in circuit expenses from next year, we agreed earlier this year to contribute a further 10% as from September 1974, which will mean paying £710. However, the rest of the circuit is paying at the rate of £10.65 per member. For us to contribute at this rate we would have to find £1480.35; our membership is 139. This is more than the (our) total income for the year ..."

The Roscoe congregation responded positively to this invitation and challenge, but like so many other churches and voluntary groups income from membership always needed to be on the increase. It was not easy for West Indian families to rise to expectations, but once the new Church was their spiritual home remarkable changes took place.

The Finance Committee meeting of 24th September 1975 was informed by the Church Treasurer, Okuro Ndukwe, that the first instalment to start repaying the outstanding loan of £1500 from the Leeds District Extension Fund was due in December. The Committee agreed to request an extension on the time for repayment due to Roscoe's financial stringency. The Methodist Church Property Division had promised a grant towards the cost of the new Church building of £750 but this would not be remitted until all other loans and bills had been met. Hence the dilemma. By September 9th 1976 Roscoe had only managed to repay £145 against the District Loan.

However, at the June 23rd 1977 Finance Committee meeting a letter from the Superintendent Minister was read out. Alan Odell requested Roscoe to consider releasing £100 of the £250 annual Home Mission grant in order to assist the Trinity congregation, which was in great need of financial assistance. The Finance Committee agreed to this. Roscoe's positive financial position by this time was substantially helped by the rental monies being received from the Citizen's Advice Bureau and the Roscoe Day Nursery.

The February 2nd 1978 Finance Meeting was reassured by Trevor Bates that the Superintendent minister, Revd Alan Odell was negotiating with the Property Division to try and get their promised grant remitted as soon as possible, and the June 8th 1978 meeting was informed that the grant of £750 had been received. The Church Treasurer told the September 7th 1978 meeting that all Roscoe's indebtedness had finally been cleared. This was due in no small measure to the congregation's positive response to the challenge for more realistic and positive weekly giving.

*Mr William Farrar Vickers with documents buried with the Foundation
Stone of Roscoe Place, May 1976*

89

EXTENSION TO THE PREMISES

By 1978 it was quite evident that serious consideration needed to be given to extending the premises of Roscoe to meet existing commitments for those who rented rooms from us and better enable them to serve the wider neighbourhood and community. In addition Roscoe folk also felt the need to provide additional facilities for their own work with children and young people.

In 1978 Leeds City Council, along with other cities in England, was developing an Inner City Programme to meet the special needs of areas where immigrant people had come to settle from many different countries. Inner city unrest in different towns and cities in the UK added urgency and priority to such new ventures. Trevor Bates shared with the Church Council of September 28th the need for an extension to our premises and how an application for funding should be made by Roscoe to Leeds City Council, under the Inner City Programme, to build an adjacent building and so help fulfil our vision.

The Church Council decided that the new building should be seen as a Community Service building, consisting of: a gymnasium, shower facilities, a spectator area, coffee bar, toilets, and an additional kitchen with a separate office suite for the Citizen's Advice Bureau and special facilities for the Roscoe Day Nursery which would enable them to move out of the Church building altogether. The estimated cost was £110,000, of which £25,000 would need to be contributed from Methodist sources, i.e. a grant of £20,000 from Methodist Connexional Funds, and £5,000 to be raised by Roscoe.

By May 1981 the Finance Committee heard from Mr John Goddard, the architect, that the cost of the new building would be £201,000 due to inflation. At that date the promised grants etc. were:

Leeds Inner City programme	£125,000
Methodist Connexional Advance Fund	£25,000
Rank Trust	£20,000
Methodist Property Division	£3,500
Leeds Methodist District Churches	£15,000
Roscoe Church	£6,950

90

There would be a shortfall of several thousand pounds, due to additional work needed in the foundations where a culvert had been discovered, this expense to be met from other sources yet to be explored.

THE OFFICIAL OPENING OF ADDITIONAL PREMISES

The Official Opening and Dedication of the new building, to be known as **Willow House** and **Roscoe Hall,** took place on Saturday 25th July 1981 in two stages: **Willow House** at 2.45pm when **Mr John Goddard**, the architect, handed over the key to **Mr Harry Cocksedge,** a long standing member and representative of the Roscoe congregation, who officially opened Willow House; this was followed by an Act of Dedication with responses led by the Superintendent Minister, the **Revd Alan J. Odell BA.**

The gathering was then asked to wait for the arrival of the Lord Mayor of Leeds **Cllr. Patrick Crotty OBE, LLB,** who along with Mr David Haley, contractor, the Revd W. Stanley Rose BD, Chairman of the Leeds Methodist District, **Revd Peter A. Kerridge** General Secretary of the Methodist Property Division, the Revd Alan J. Odell and Revd Trevor S. Bates assembled at the front door to **Roscoe Hall.** At 3.15pm Mr David Haley handed over the front door key to **the Lord Mayor** who then officially opened the door of Roscoe Hall. **The Revd Stanley Rose** led an Act of Dedication with responses. The whole gathering went into Roscoe Hall where a service was conducted by Revd Trevor S. Bates with greetings and addresses being given by the Lord Mayor, Revd Peter Kerridge, Revd Stanley Rose and Revd Alan Odell. Mr Arthur Saddler, local preacher and member of Roscoe, read scripture lessons and Mr Cedric Clarke, Senior Church Steward, gave a word of thanks.

The **Citizens Advice Bureau and their Tribunal Unit** quickly moved out of the Church building into Willow House, and the **Roscoe Day Nursery** moved out of the Fellowship Room into Roscoe Hall and the Conservatory area. Overnight the congestion which had been the cause of many difficulties was eased and our tenants were delighted with the new facilities.

91

Involvement in the wider community may be illustrated by those of Roscoe's congregation who became **JPs** - **Mrs Diana Phillip (1969), Mr John Connor (1981), Mr George Eubanks (1982) and Mr Cedric Clarke (1985)**. Trevor Bates served on the Leeds Community Relations Council, and the Management Committees of the Chapeltown Adventure Playground and Chapeltown CAB; Curlita Kelly became Secretary of the Chapeltown Churches Association, and two members served on the CAB Management Committee. Several members also supported the Leeds Concord Inter-Faith Fellowship which was started in 1976. **Arthur France**, pioneer of the Chapeltown Carnival, and **Hughbon Condor**, inspired creator of Carnival costumes, are also members of Roscoe Church.

It is also worthwhile to remember that the **Revd Kenneth Glendinning,** who served Roscoe as a probationer 1967/68 with Revd J Malcolm Furness, then became minister for Trinity and Ashley Road Churches before being appointed as **Senior Community Relations Officer** for Leeds 1975 – 81. In many ways Roscoe Methodist Church was becoming the hub of activity in Leeds working for ethnic and community harmony.

The Revd Trevor Bates left in August 1981 to be Superintendent of the Pudsey and Farsley circuit. Working with Trevor during his nine year period with Roscoe were: **Probationers**: Revd Ian G. Lucraft BA (1972-74), Revd Raymond Garfoot BA (1974-75). **Deaconesses**: Sister Lily Dobbs (1975-76) and Sister Margaret Horn (1976-82), who remained to continue with Trevor's successor, the **Revd John Whittle BD**.

It needs to be recorded that the total transformation and relocation of both congregation and premises from the Roscoe Place (Wesleyan Chapel) Methodist Church site in Sheepscar to the present location of on the site of historic Willow House home of Benjamin Randall Vickers, was the result of vision and team work across many years. The investment of Leeds City Council and of the Methodist Church and people at different levels together with the dedicated involvement by ministers, deaconesses and lay folk of the Roscoe congregation, particularly in the post WWII years, has resulted in a set of premises and an ongoing programme of vibrant activity serving the neighbourhood and wider community of Leeds in the name of Christ.

Roscoe Boys' Brigade Officers and Chaplain, 1977

Roscoe Girls' Brigade Officers with District Commissioner, 1975

Roscoe Girls' Brigade Company with Officers, Chaplain, and District Commissioner, 1975

95

REMINISCENCES FIVE

SURE AND STEADFAST

AS A YOUNG CHILD growing up in St Kitts (Caribbean), I was a member of the Boys' Brigade and its motto "Sure and Steadfast" and the Anchor Song "Will your anchor hold in storms of life", left an indelible impression on me and has been the guiding principle on how to live my life.

When I lived with my Grandmother Henrietta Walters, there was never a question of not attending church every Sunday unless I was ill, and thankfully I have been well most of my life. My Mum, Rebecca Condor, ensured that the same principle continued when I came to England and even reminded me the week after I got married in the New Roscoe Church (a week after it was opened) that she still expected to see me in church every Sunday, something I continue to do with great regularity.

The late Mr George Eubanks, using his persuasive powers created an image of what things could be like and persuaded me to take up my first appointment in the church as a Boys' Brigade officer. Mr Eubanks was the Captain and I joined the ranks with fellow officers Mr Alan Herbert, Ms Hillary Podd and my brother and sister Leroy Condor and Patsy Claxton to form and restart the 13th Leeds Boys' Brigade in the new Roscoe Church.

Later, Mr Eubanks handed over the role of Church Secretary to me, which I did for more than a decade. It is easy to attend church on Sunday without being involved in the church and it sometimes requires a light bulb moment to realise that being a Christian is more that attending the Sunday Service. It occurred to me that in our church there was the absence of Bible study. I can even remember thinking why we are spending money to furnish the church with Bibles when we don't appear to read them. It was a topic of many discussions on numerous occasions that we should have a Bible Study class. Eventually, a period of Bible study was led by the minister for a short time. At the end of the period, we were at risk of reverting back to a void of studying the Bible in our church on a regular basis. It felt like going to the gym and just getting into being fit, only to be told 'that's it', until some unspecified period time in the future. The light bulb moment came when I almost involuntarily put my hand up and said that I will lead the Bible classes. This I have been able to do fortnightly, since 2005, with the occasional absence, as my anchor held during the many storms that I faced during this period when it would have been easy to give up and discontinue with the Bible Studies. The rocks that held my anchor were the senior members of our church that gave me encouragement by their regular attendance.

Becoming a Church Steward and eventually the Senior Steward was another one of those moments that seems to just happen, I volunteered without consciously doing it. My wife Gloria was a steward before me and so I had a pretty good idea of the time commitment that was necessary to do the role effectively. I felt that I couldn't take it on because I was too busy doing the things that I enjoyed doing. Then it occurred to me, should I not show my gratitude for my life by giving up some of my time for the work of God? It became an easy decision to justify. This was further reinforced during one of our Bible Studies, when we looked at things in our lives that could be considered as being in competition with God, in effect, things that we may unknowingly worship and can't do without. I needed to know if making carnival costumes was that other God for me. When it was my turn to fulfil the role of Senior Steward I knew this was the test as it meant that I had to decide on doing carnival or the role of Senior Steward. Thankfully, I made the right decision and took time out from carnival.

Looking ahead, hopefully there will be further challenges for me in the life of our church, and with the help of God I will remain 'Sure and Steadfast' and continue to 'Hold on God's Anchor'.

Hughbon Condor

A REFLECTION OF MY TIME AT ROSCOE METHODIST CHURCH

I FIRST ATTENDED Roscoe Place Methodist Church in 1966, after I came to England with my twin sister, Judith from Nevis, to join our parents, James and Etheline Weekes. We were taken to church by Mum, who was a strong and committed Christian. My first impression of the church was its age, architecture and stained glass windows, which was very different from the church I attended in Nevis. From the outset we were made very welcome by the members, including the late Mr & Mrs Lunn and their daughter Dorothy, Elsie Plumb and Mrs Atkinson. The Minister at that time was Rev Malcolm Furness.

My sister and I were confirmed as full members of the church in December 1970 by Rev Michael Chapman and Rev Peter Williamson. The church was a vibrant place in which to worship and had many activities for young people, including a youth club and a summer play scheme which was held for two weeks during the school holidays. These were started by the late Rev Kenneth Glendinning, a trainee minister at the time. Sunday School was also very active and was held in the afternoons.

A memorable event that took place was the filming of one of our Christmas Sunday Services, which was filmed by Yorkshire Television. My sister Judith played the role of Mary. This was received positively by the community and many viewers, although there were some negative comments from people who said the role of Mary should not have been portrayed by a black person.

A new road development led to the demolition of the old church and a new one was built on Francis Street named Roscoe Methodist Church. The new church was designed to function on several levels: attached is the Citizens Advice Bureau and a Day Nursery which was run by Mrs Notay (the Nursery has since closed). Following concerns raised by members to the Minister, Rev Trevor Bates and Sister Margaret Horn, the West Indian Family Counselling Service (WIFCOS) was formed in September 1979. A committee was formed and I became the Secretary and remained in that post for many years. I also worked with the Minister, Rev Trevor Bates and others including the late Mr Arthur Saddler and Mr Roland Lunn in the appointment of its first worker, Mr Emmanuel Kebbe. However he left the post within a year and Mrs Mary Saddler was appointed as his successor. WIFCOS obtained funding from the Joseph Rowntree Charitable Trust in York, who supported it for two years. Funding was also gained from other charities, including the NCH.

I later became involved in other work within the life of the church, including assisting with the Sunday School and typing the weekly church bulletin. I became a Communion Steward in 2000 and then Senior Communion Steward in 2001 (a role I took over from Mrs Joyce Jobson who left to join her family in America). I stood down from this role in May 2010. I am currently the Secretary for the Finance and Property Committee and the Property Sub-Group, positions which I have held for several years.

I married Lennie Jeffers at Roscoe on 2nd July 1983 and the service was conducted by Rev John Whittle. We have two children, Helen and Nathan, who were both christened at Roscoe by Sister Stella Bullivant.

Sadly my parents passed away in July 2009, within five days of each other. Their funeral services were held at Roscoe. The family greatly appreciated the support, kindness and fellowship offered by the members of the church and the community during this difficult time.

As a member of the congregation I have witnessed many changes within our church, the community and the world around us, which continues to change. One thing that never changes, though, is God's love for us and I will continue to serve him.

Joan Jeffers

THE NDUKWE FAMILY
AND ROSCOE METHODIST CHURCH

OKORO AND OYIDIA NDUKWE were married on March 10th 1973 at the old Roscoe Place Methodist Church. They had got engaged just before Okoro came to England in 1962 on a scholarship to do chartered accountancy. Oyidia had been educated in a Methodist school in Nigeria and had done just one year at Teacher Training College when her studies were interrupted by the outbreak of the Biafran war. She was finally able to join Okoro in Leeds in December 1972.

99

After seeing an advertisement in *The Methodist Recorder* they volunteered to work abroad, sponsored by the Overseas Division of the Methodist Church. After four months at Selly Oak Missionary Training College in Birmingham, where Revd George Lovell was a tutor, they flew to Katmandu from Yeadon Airport in January 1981, to serve in Nepal with their three young children, Ndukwe (known as Endie) aged 6, Nenna, who was nearly 4 and Kalu aged 2. Roscoe church members and the then minister, Revd Trevor Bates, had supported the Ndukwes' calling to go and serve abroad and they organised a grand farewell party for them at Roscoe followed by a special circuit service at Lidgett Park Methodist Church .

Initially the children attended the British International Primary School in Katmandu as Okoro and Oyidiya had to attend a language school before starting work in Butwal, a village in the foothills of Mount Everest. Okoro worked as a business manager with the District Economic Development Board of the United Mission to Nepal which ran a hydro-electric scheme to provide electricity for the rural areas.

When they left Nepal in 1986 the secretary wrote, "On the mission field one is often called upon to do much more than expected. Oyidiya has the gift of Christian hospitality and has kept the door open for friends and colleagues, the needy and estranged, as well as teaching her own children and those of her colleagues. We shall long remember her dedicated Christian faith and devotion to others." The Ndukwes spent five years serving the Lord in Nepal. While on furlough in the UK they were invited to various circuits to talk about their work. In February 1986 they were among a group of expatriates selected to meet the Queen and the Duke of Edinburgh, who were visiting Nepal.

On their return to the UK the family rejoined Roscoe Methodist Church. Over the years Okoro used his skills as an accountant in serving as Church Treasurer and he later became Senior Church Steward. Sadly for the church and the Ndukwe family, he passed away on May 20th 2001 after a short battle with cancer. He is remembered by the church family at Roscoe for his services, faith and wisdom.

Oyidiya joined the church choir and became Envelope Secretary for our planned giving scheme. More recently she was commissioned as a worship   leader. Nenna taught   in   Sunday School and Kalu is   a Communion Steward. Endie has continued to attend services at Roscoe during visits from his home in Harrogate and now in south Leeds.

In 2008 the Ndukwe family and Roscoe Church held a celebration party for Nenna on completion of her doctorate in clinical psychology. Similarly, two years later, church members provided a warm send off for Nenna as she left to work at the James Cook University Hospital in Singapore.

There is something wonderful about Roscoe Methodist Church which holds many happy memories for the Ndukwe family.

Mr Okuru and Mrs Oyidiya Ndukwe with their three children prior to departure for overseas service in Nepal, January 1981

101

INFORMATION ABOUT HISTORY OF ROSCOE METHODIST CHURCH

WHEN TRAVELLING from Leeds City Centre up Chapeltown Road the Roscoe Place Methodist Church was situated on your right and St.Clements Anglican Church stood directly opposite it on the left.

In the early 60's it was always admirable to see the congregation of both churches going into or coming from worship. The majority were West Indians, and the children were prettily dressed, adding lots of colour to the old stone buildings. Vividly I remember going to a couple of Emancipation Services conducted by the late Revd Wm. Sunter (*who lived and worked in the Leeward Islands District for many years*). I also attended a few baptisms/christenings and one of the most beautiful summer weddings there too.

Eventually the church moved to Francis Street in the 70s and I moved from South Leeds to be nearer the church. This was a pleasurable opportunity to attend the new Roscoe Church regularly. With a large congregation of mainly West Indian families and a minister who I knew since back home in the islands. I felt very much at home there, even though the building was an entirely modern church.

Roscoe Church has had many changes but it is still firmly standing on its "Spiritual Foundation" as a testimony that Jesus Christ is Lord! Roscoe Church has played a very fulfilling and outstanding role in the community. The Church is very well used for all sorts of useful and necessary functions and projects which serve the needs of the multicultural residents. I hope that my memories will help to complete the history, and that everyone can be proud of their Christian life and participation in such a renowned and remarkable church within the heart of Chapeltown and Harehills.

Clarita Wenham

MEMORIES

I CAN REMEMBER THE OLD Roscoe Church because I used to attend on special occasions. After we were married at the new Roscoe Church in 1981, my husband and I began to attend the new Roscoe regularly. One disappointment was that new members and visitors to the church did not receive a warm welcome on Sunday mornings. After discussing this with the minister and the younger members of the church we decided to form a young members group called 'Dare to Share'. One of the decisions we made was to have a welcoming group on Sunday mornings that would greet the congregation; this was a great success and it is still providing a greeting at the door to this day.

We also thought that the church was lacking a singing group. It was left to me to get up in church one Sunday morning to ask if anyone would like to join a singing group. I managed to get a group started consisting of men and women of all ages. We asked Mr St Clair Morris if he would tutor the group and he agreed. Mr Morris also provided our unique steel pan accompaniment. We called the group the Roscoe Singers and the group is still going today after many years. We have sung at various churches in the circuit and at special events in the local community and further afield.

Angela Wenham

Chapter Six

INTO THE 21ˢᵗ CENTURY
1981 - 2010

A NEW MINISTER

The Revd John Whittle, who had recently returned to England from service in the Leeward Islands District in the West Indies, took up his post at Roscoe Methodist Church in September 1981. Assisting him in ministry was **Deaconess Margaret Horn**, who was already in post from 1976. They worked well together and instigated new ideas during their time of service at Roscoe. Sister Margaret left in 1982 and was then replaced by **Sister Stella Bullivant** who remained until 1990 when she retired. **Sister Eileen Gaunt**, who hailed from the Roscoe congregation, retired in 1980 and came to live in Chapeltown until her death in 1996. During those years Sister Eileen was a very active member in Roscoe's life.

Because this book includes the reminiscences of former members of the congregation, ministers and deaconesses, which convey vital pictures of this contemporary period, we here briefly summarize some of the concerns and achievements of Roscoe's life.

MINISTRY WITH CHILDREN AND YOUNG PEOPLE

Sunday School: In March 1982 the Sunday School session was moved to the morning, when the children shared the first few minutes of the Morning Service then left to go to their own classes. At the end of the classes the children were re-united with the main service. This meant that there was no need for a separate afternoon session. It was noted that the attendance improved.

Baptisms: The practice in connection with the Sacrament of Baptism was reviewed, because of concerns raised about attitudes displayed during the service. Pre-baptismal explanations were given to the parents, re the baptismal water, the offering of the candle, and the vows made. Baptisms of babies and small children continue and efforts are made to visit the homes of these baptised children, especially on the occasion of their birthdays. The parents are sent special invitations to Christmas, Mothering Sunday and Father's Day services which some of the parents accept.

Saturday School: During John Whittle's ministry, a Saturday School was started at Roscoe, in partnership with Trinity and All Saints College of Leeds. This was to help the children with their education. The attendance was between 50 and 60 each week. The School continued for some time.

Mothers' and Toddlers' Club: A Mothers' & Toddlers' Club, which was started during Sister Margaret's time at Roscoe, was also successful for a number of years.

Youth Fellowship: A Youth Fellowship started by the **Revd David Whitehall** and his wife **Mandy**, went on for a while.

Summer Play Scheme: In 1982 for the benefit of children of the community as a whole a Summer Play Scheme was co-ordinated by Sister Margaret (who was a trained teacher). The staff also had to have teaching qualifications and we were fortunate to have **Miss Hilary Podd** and **Miss Patsy Condor** to help when necessary. Children were invited to Roscoe during their summer school holidays, when supervised activities and outings were organised for them. Two such outings were visits to Golden Acre Park and Bradford Ice Rink. The scheme continued during Sister Stella's time at Roscoe, but had to close when it became difficult to find other teachers to volunteer.

Roscoe Day Nursery: The Roscoe Day Nursery which opened in 1976 with **Mrs Oma Notay** as organiser, closed in March 2006 due to lack of funding to maintain the staff required for the number of children being cared for.

FINANCE

Giving: Church members are encouraged to be regular weekly givers, and to put aside their offering for the Sundays when they don't attend church, bringing it with them, when they do. Members and other givers who are tax payers, are encouraged to Gift-Aid. This means that for every £1.00 donated, the Church is given 28p from the tax-man, as at January 2011.

Reducing Circuit Staff Costs: As a way of reducing the cost of staff, the Leeds North East circuit decided not to replace the Deaconess, Sister Stella, on her retirement in 1990. This left the minister as the only staff member for Roscoe.

VISITORS

Caribbean: In August 1982 Roscoe welcomed special visitors on a Methodist Church Youth Exchange Programme from the Caribbean. They were here for about five days, were accommodated by Roscoe and visited other churches during their stay. This was a great success.

Birmingham: Roscoe Methodist Church and Sparkhill Methodist Church, Birmingham, arranged exchange visits between them, and had two such effective visits by groups from each church in the 1970s.

MORE COMMUNITY SCHEMES

Street Wardens: In 1983, the Chapeltown and Harehills Churches Together, of which Roscoe is a member, was awarded a grant of £9000 to set up a Street Warden Scheme. This was to encourage cross cultural community care in the area, by encouraging people to communicate and help one another, regardless of ethnic origin. Mrs Celia Greenwell from Social Services was the Co-ordinator, and Mrs Millicent Francis with Mrs Mary Saddler of Roscoe were members of the Management Committee.

Mr Richard Pinder was also involved and Mr Charles Ward, a resident of Chapeltown, was appointed Warden. The scheme ran for about two years with some success.

Prostitute Field Worker: At a special Roscoe Church Council meeting on 16th April 1989, it was agreed to support the proposal for a Prostitution Field Worker. This was to become a project of the Chapeltown and Harehills Churches Association, under the Chairmanship of Revd John Howard, minister at Trinity Church,

106

Roundhay Road. Members of Roscoe were on the Committee and, when the project developed, it became known as GENESIS. Its aim was to be alongside of women of all ages, who were involved in, or wished to leave, prostitution within the Leeds area. The project provides information, support and advocacy, and now has its office at Oxford Chambers, Oxford Place, Leeds.

Chapeltown Laundry: During March 1983 the Chapeltown Laundry Co-op was opened on the corner of Mexborough Avenue and Chapeltown Road to fill a need in the community. It was managed and run by women from Roscoe and the community – **Millicent Francis, Mary Saddler, Frances Skelton and Myrna Tyrell**, with **Tessa Francis, Judy Thorpe, Veronica Rose and Georgina Webbe** whilst Sister Stella gave pastoral support by visiting and encouragement. It closed in 1995 after giving 12 years of dedicated service to the people of Chapeltown.

Roscoe Luncheon Club: Mary Saddler of The West Indian Family Counselling Service initiated the Roscoe Luncheon Club in 1983 which meets on Tuesdays and Thursdays with one paid and several volunteer members of staff. Over the years **Stephanie Lewis, Carol Stapleton, Joyce Vernon, Eunice French, Kathy Douglas** and others have been workers The Luncheon Club remains a popular service to this day.

Cllr. Norma Hutchinson was a very lively Ward Councillor and a member of Roscoe. In 1991 she became the first Jamaican to serve on Leeds City Council and remained so until her premature death in 2004 at the age of 55 years. Norma was dynamically active for people and issues in the Chapeltown and Harehills areas.

CHURCH ANNIVERSARY CELEBRATIONS

The 10th and 25th Anniversaries of the new Church were occasions for special celebration. For the **10th Anniversary – 7th October 1984** - Trevor Bates willingly accepted the invitation to be guest preacher for that day. However in 1999, for the **25th Anniversary** celebrations, the entire month of October – five Sundays – were occasions for guest preachers and special thanksgiving. Revd Michael Townsend, then Chairman of the Leeds District, Revd John Whittle, Revd Peter

107

Reasbeck, Revd Trevor Bates, Revd Ian Lucraft, Sister Margaret Horn and Sister Stella Bullivant together with Revd Robert Creamer, Mr John Connor and Mr Arthur Saddler all shared in leading worship during that month of rejoicing.

CHANGES IN MINISTERIAL STAFF

Sharing: Roscoe Methodist and Woodhouse Methodist Churches, shared the same minister for a number of years, starting with Michael Chapman in 1970 until Robert Creamer moved out of the circuit (2006).The two Churches shared services, and jointly attended Cliff College Anniversary Celebration weekends several times. In 2006 the twelve churches in the Leeds North East circuit were re-aligned and the ministers reduced from 6 to 5. Roscoe and Trinity United Church on Roundhay Road now share the same minister. **Mary Saddler**, a member of Roscoe, works with the Revd Mark Harwood as the Pastoral Support Worker for Trinity United Church.

Departure and coverage: In 1984 John Whittle was invited to serve a further term at Roscoe, but in February 1985 he announced his intending departure in August that year. The Revd Peter Reasbeck, being the Superintendent for Leeds North East Circuit, temporarily became minister for Roscoe and Woodhouse Churches in September 1985 with the expectation that a new minister would take up post in September 1986. However, the Revd Graham Kent, who was stationed to the circuit, was unable to take up the appointment which meant that Peter Reasbeck continued coverage until August 1987. The Deaconess, Sister Stella played a vital part in the ministry of these two churches, especially in this intervening period.

The **Revd David Whitehall** was welcomed in September 1987 and was with us until 1992. In 1990 the treasurer of Roscoe, Albertha Freeman, resigned and David Whitehall acted as treasurer. Later that year Yvonne Herbert took up the post and remained treasurer until 2004. In 1992 the **Revd Robert B. Creamer** was appointed as minister for Roscoe. He and his wife Revd Pat Creamer and their two children were warmly welcomed and Robert remained for 14 years.

The **Revd Mark Harwood** is the present minister for Roscoe Methodist Church and Trinity United Church. We welcomed him and his wife Hazel and family in September 2006 and we have invited him to remain in this appointment for another term, which he has accepted. The Gledhow Park manse, which Mark Harwood and family occupy, was updated and extended in 2009, at a cost of £35,000.

DUTIES AND RESPONSIBILITIES

Members not volunteering to be responsible for specific duties in the Church was an ongoing concern. Ministers and deaconesses over the years tried to persuade and encourage them to have self-confidence, but it was not until Robert Creamer was the minister that this commitment became more successful *(see Robert Creamer's 'Reminiscences')*. Also in Robert Creamer's time, the issue of members not knowing/speaking and socialising with one another in the Church, was discussed. Efforts made to try to improve this attitude resulted in some success, and are ongoing.

SUPPORT FOR THE BEREAVED

Ministers and deaconesses observed the **seriousness** with which West Indians coped with bereavement, not only within their own families, but also other members of the community even those who were not personally known to them. As a result in 1997 a Bereavement Support Group was started at Roscoe *(See Robert Creamer's 'Reminiscences')*

GENERAL UPDATING OF CHURCH

Internal – Furniture and Books: In order to increase the warmth of the Church, the worship area and the foyer were carpeted wall to wall. Over the years as the original chairs, which were plastic, began to break when in use, they were replaced by wooden, padded comfortable chairs, which matched the carpet.

New hymn books (*Hymns and Psalms*) and the *Complete Edition of Mission Praise* were bought, and for the first time, bibles, which remained in the Church. These Good News Bibles are placed on the shelves of the chairs, ready for use by the congregation, adults and children.

Building problems: Over the years, the most compelling and recurring expenses were due to the problems caused as a result of the original flat roof of the Church building. David Whitehall and Robert Creamer, with the Property Committee, have dealt with recurrent and expensive repairs to the roof. At last in 2009/2010 with our present minister, Mark Harwood, we have seen this problem solved.

The building now has a new roof at a cost of £98,500. This was raised by a combination of Ms Dorothy Ramsden's Bequest of £18,000, a Leeds City Council Grant of £20,000 together with fund raising and reserves of £60,500; which included repaying a loan of £20,000 from the Leeds District Methodist Extension Society. The new roof includes six large sky-light windows over the worship area, letting in not only plenty of daylight but also rays of sunshine!

Outside repairs to the building are carried out as necessary and the garden at the front of the Church *(on Chapeltown Road)* was landscaped *(See Robert Creamer's 'Reminiscences')*. Additional lighting and the improvement of the sound system were also carried out.

MEMBERSHIP

In Methodism 'Membership' is the list of those who have formally become members of the Church by commitment and can therefore take a full and active part. There will be many others who are part of the life of the church without being formal 'members' *(known as 'Adherents')*. In 1987 the membership of Roscoe was 164. As at 30th October 2010 membership was 126.

ROSCOE – A COMMUNITY CHURCH

Roscoe Methodist Church, in the community of Chapeltown, continues to welcome people of all nationalities, from within this country and overseas. Other Christian groups continue to use some of our rooms for their own services, thus worshipping God according to their own tradition and culture. The premises have also been used by the Sickle Cell Society, the St Kitts/Nevis Association and Police and Commmunity Together (PACT) meetings, among others.

RIOTING IN THE COMMUNITY

The dissatisfaction with conditions in Chapeltown, and racism, which were the experience of many, culminated in the violence and burning down of businesses and other buildings in the community on Bonfire Night 1975, and again in July 1981.

Unemployment, particularly among young people, was very high, and that generation, unlike their parents, was far less inclined to accept the way things were. Like other inner-city areas, e.g. Brixton and Bristol, riots and uprising took place but were not as widespread in Leeds. The impact of these riots are still evident to those who lived through them, but there have been a lot of improvements.

It was said that although a variety of buildings were destroyed, Roscoe Methodist Church was untouched, because of the service it gives to the community as a whole.

WE GRATEFULLY REMEMBER

The people who arrived in Leeds from the Caribbean in the late fifties and early sixties found life very difficult. They were working long hours, often on shifts, and living conditions were poor. They had high hopes for their children but the British education system often seemed to fail them. Members of the Chapeltown community fought hard to combat racism and unintended stereotyping in schools.

Over the years young people from Roscoe have overcome these hurdles and have carved out successful careers in education, the arts, social services, etc. becoming role models for the Afro-Caribbean community.

Across the years depicted in our history many people, members and friends of Roscoe Methodist Church, from 1862 to the present day have served the community by being involved with this Church. It is impossible to name them all, but they are not forgotten. Their witness is

111

our heritage in the faith of Christ. To them, therefore, we say thank you for your loyal service and generous commitment. With Joseph Hart we join with one voice:

"We'll praise God for all that is past
And trust Him for all that's to come"

Roscoe Girls' Brigade with District Commissioner, 2000

REMINISCENCES SIX

REMINISCENCES OF ROSCOE

THE ANNUAL SUNDAY SCHOOL OUTING was always an event we looked forward to. I remember in the early 70's we went to places like South Milford nr Selby when Roland Lunn was the Superintendent of the Sunday School. However by the late 1970s and early 80s we were venturing further afield to places like Southport and Morecambe. There would sometimes be a church hall in the vicinity that we would perhaps descend on in order to get refreshments. I am sure that this was arranged with the receiving church prior to us turning up. It was a sure bet that Mrs Pennycooke would be late boarding the coach when leaving Roscoe for the trip. However it was taken in good spirits and strangely enough it would not have felt like the Sunday School outing if she was on time!

Looking back I think that Sunday school was remarkably successful in its day. We are talking about an era before VCR, CDs and of course the Internet. I remember Mr Connor and Mr Saddler leading it. I then graduated to the senior class and that was led by Ms Sanders and her guitar! The Sunday School would also organize the Christmas parties which I thoroughly enjoyed.

Looking back at the Youth Club of the late 70s early 80s it was a crucible of many interesting ideas and formats. Stephen Woodley and I, for example, would write small plays and perform them. Oddly we never gave ourselves a name but we performed in a few locations. These plays were fun but with a Christian message. The PA system for many of these events was provided by a small electronics company based in Headingley that Stephen worked for. We would also participate in social events at Roscoe. After all there was a stage provided in the church so why not?

The youth of the church would also take part in the MAYC weekend in London. This is where Methodist Youth Clubs from all over the UK would travel to London to take part in 'London weekend' with the culmination being a service at the Royal Albert Hall on a Sunday morning in May. In this way we met other youth clubs and people from around the country. We would normally join up with the youth club in Chapel Allerton to do this.

In 1983 I was happy and proud to represent Roscoe when I was selected to go on a Youth Exchange with young people from other churches in the UK to the USA and the Caribbean. Upon my return, I travelled through Yorkshire showing pictures and telling others of my experiences with other Methodist Young people around the world. It was a fantastic experience.

Does anyone remember collecting old newspaper? Mr Cocksedge was in charge. I never understood how it worked - I must have been 12 or 13 at the time but occasionally Mr Cocksedge would organise paper collections which I understand would be converted into cash for the church.

I have a memory of being in a caged van and being up to my eyeballs in newspaper!

Andrew Clarke

MEMORIES OF AN ORGANIST

ONE SUNDAY IN MARCH, 1977, Roscoe Methodist Church did a national broadcast live for ITV. For weeks there had been much excitement in anticipation of the great day. As a 13 year old and an organist of a mere few months, the whole prospect filled me more with trepidation than anything else. The Minister, Revd Trevor Bates, had chosen the hymns in good time so I had plenty of opportunity to get the tunes well and truly under my fingers; I had to as I had been chosen to play for the morning worship broadcast over the other three young, teenage organist who also played at Roscoe Church—much to the disquiet of their parents.

On the Saturday prior to the broadcast, there was a technical rehearsal at the church— the place was a veritable hive of activity full of people both strange and familiar making themselves of use, whether required or not. The programme director was extremely easy to work with and we only needed to run through the script once. I stayed behind to practise in what seemed like a very darkened environment after the dazzling light of the TV lanterns. The Choirmaster, Mr Harris, and the Caretaker, Mr Connor, were there to do some final preparations before the big day. I made a recording of some parts of my practice which, unbelievably, still exists!! I remember taking it home, playing it through and analysing it.

The following day, the broadcast went very smoothly indeed; everything went according to the script, the timing was spot on (although I did receive a letter from a gentleman from York who was saddened that there wasn't enough time to hear the whole of my organ voluntary at the end of the service), the singing was hearty, everyone was in their very best 'bib and tucker' (one lady's hat was so big and ostentatious that she virtually blocked the view of a third of all the rows directly behind her). For my own part, I don't remember making any mistakes and, judging by the letters I received and the response from teachers and pupils at school, all my practice and preparation had paid off.

As I left the church that Sunday morning with my mother, a member of the congregation stopped us and told my mother 'He did well this morning— you must be proud'. On hearing this, my mother cried.

Mervyn Williams MA FTCL ARCM NPQH FRSA
(Organist: 1976-79)

MEMORIES OF ROSCOE

MY FONDEST MEMORIES OF ROSCOE were as a young child during Sunday School. The birthday presentations would fill me with such happiness as every child would receive a Ladybird book of famous bible stories which simply introduced young minds to the teachings of the bible. Elsie Plumb was the leading Sunday School teacher. Her kind smiling face that greeted you and her warm nature made being in Sunday School a pleasant and happy experience. The Christmas parties were fantastic— everyone was involved and the main church was filled with screaming happy children but always the main message was one of

115

Christianity which has stayed with me throughout my life and has helped shape who I have become as a person.

As the years moved on Roscoe was evolving into the most popular Methodist church within the community. It had a high population of West Indian families from the Caribbean Islands, many of whom have remained within the church. The young members, I believe, were the hub of the church. They would partake in organising the social events to raise funds for the church. What a talented group of members, dancers, musicians, choreographers! It was amazing! I was asked to perform a dance with a group of friends on Easter Sunday. It was a challenge but we danced to Boney M's 'Rivers of Babylon' dressed all in white. The congregation were ecstatic and the applause rang out and we were asked to perform again. I felt so lifted and happy. It was the first time a dance was performed on the pulpit.

The youth club was very popular and many relationships and friendships were formed. The supervisors occasionally would find it difficult trying to maintain order at the club. Mr Saddler and Mr Connor were strong leaders: you would not risk disrespecting them, which was a healthy respect, but on some occasions the boys would be mischievous, throwing snowballs and playing practical jokes, but with no malice.

I was appointed the flag bearer for the Girls' Brigade which was an honour. The girls were predominately black and this made us a focus at parades; Roscoe in the early 80's hosted the parade where all the various brigades around the region came to parade through the streets of Chapeltown and the whole community came out. I was nervous but what an experience!

Roscoe has been the foundation of my learning. My family was christened there, my mother's funeral service took place there and my brother and sister had their communion as did I. There is much photographic evidence and cinema movies of the old and present Roscoe churches with those that have come and gone, I can remember them as well as yesterday. Roscoe was renowned for the large family outings that were well attended—not just your ordinary potted beef sandwiches but fried chicken and journey cakes/bakes with doving pots full of curry goat with rice, Hornsey was the first place Roscoe members went. What a sight we were when we pulled up!

I would like to say that one thing I cannot forget about Roscoe is its Ministers and Deaconesses. Give Thanks.

Diana Woodley

MEMORIES OF ROSCOE

SO....MY MEMORIES AT ROSCOE, wow there are so many, where to begin, but here goes:

1. I'm ashamed in some ways to say that when the 13th Boys' Brigade staged 'Miss Roscoe' for charity, I won 2 years in a row, ha ha.

2. The Sunday school trips to Cleethorpes, Blackpool, Scarborough, Filey, Whitley Bay. Bridlington to Skegness, to name but a few.

3. Particularly, I remember one Sunday school trip to, I think it was, Bridlington in 1976 still the hottest summer to date, there was a ladybird epidemic. I was unfortunate enough to be stuck at a bus stop having lunch with my Mum, brothers and sisters when the influx arrived. Everyone else managed to get up and out from under the shelter where they had congregated apart from me. I was frozen solid and terrified! My mum and sister were telling me to jump over them, but still I could not. Eventually, I managed to, but not before they all took off! Hence why still to this day I have a slight phobia of the little creatures, ha ha.

4. The half-term and summer play schemes, where we would mix studies with play, watching on video for the first time then the new MTV of Sister Sledge, Diana Ross and various other artistes arranged and recorded by the then Patsy Condor.

5. The Boys' Brigade workshops we would have with Stephen Woodley, one in particular, when he asked Mark Crumbie, my brother Henroy and I to dismantle an old record player each, however we wanted. Mark Crumbie and myself proceeded to jump up and down on

117

the forsaken instrument until it was in bits, while Henroy got a screw driver and carefully dismantled and catalogued every piece. Imagine our surprise when Stephen said, "Right, now I'd like for you to put it back together". Ha ha of course Mark and I had no chance, Henry had plenty! This teaching was a valuable lesson that destruction is not the way forward. A wonderful lesson and great session.

6. The production Lisa Stephens, Michelle James, Sharon James, Julie and Richard Clarke, Honora, Annette Tyrell and myself did called 'London to York' arranged by Eileen? I can't remember her surname, but just remember it being a recital using the sounds of a train in our chant while talking about a journey from London to York. This was another great performance.

7. When my 7' foot cousin Sybil came to visit from Nevis and had to duck to get through Roscoe doors, and everyone not being able to concentrate on the sermon, due to the sheer height of her, subsequently us taking a picture after the service, with her, my mum, brothers and sisters, only to find that when we developed the picture, her head had been cut off the top of the frame. Very funny indeed!

8. The summer trip myself, Honora, Henroy and various others had, arranged by Roscoe to a place called Bramhope, where we stayed for a whole week, having to date, THE BEST TIME OF MY LIFE, doing obstacle courses, orienteering, treasure hunts, and much more. A real bonding time for all involved.

9. My mother's funeral and being so dumb struck and honoured at the turn out for her send off, so much so that the church could not hold the capacity, and people being in the foyer and the street! By the way I am crying tears of joy and thanks as I type this bit!

10. Being honoured to always be a part of Hughbon Condor's Carnival Troupe. Every year it won both best Carnival Queen and Troupe.

11. The harvest celebrations, when every member of the church would get a basket of crops to take home, at the time I didn't realise how symbolic it was!

12. The Charity Christmas gifts, my mum would bring home donated by the church, as times were hard and she struggled to boy us presents for said occasion.

13. The 'Bring and Buy' sales.

14. The fact that we would always have someone we knew dressing up as Father Christmas, and each year we would try and guess who the person was. I love that!

15. The sense of belonging to a community, without even really realising it.

16. Auntie Jean's wonderful laugh and endless positive cheery disposition.

17. The choir practice I would hear after evening service waiting for my mum.

18. On one of those occasions while waiting for my mum, I would roam the church, looking for something to occupy my time with. One evening, me being the inquisitive, mischievous child that I was, I thought it would be a good idea to see what would happen if I took the pin out of the fire extinguisher that used to reside in the corridor to the back. To my surprise, now I don't remember if I actually pressed the handle or not but, it fired out an almighty blast of continuous water. Preceeded by John Connor or Mr Saddler running through to stop it before it flooded the church. When asked what happened, I'm ashamed to say that the first thing that came into my head was, "I was just walking down the corridor and it just went off and fired at me" (Please forgive me for that white lie, Mum!), but as they say confessions are good for the soul, so here after 30 years it is! In bold black and white and for all of Roscoe to hear! Sorry Mr Saddler and Auntie Jean!

19. Of course last but not least, the honour, although I had no idea at the time, of being the first baby christened at the new Roscoe in 1973! (1974?)

I could probably go on and on if I really thought some more, but suffice to say that Roscoe had a huge impact, in terms of support, joy, laughter and tears of shaping the person I am today, and I am proud to have been a part of it. I hope this helps, and I hope I am able to perform for you guys on that wonderful occasion.

Jason Pennycooke

(PS: Hi ,
Please forgive me cutting the call short on the 23rd when you called. I was in the middle of a practice pitch with 600 kids, doing the final tech for a Guinness World Record, to have the most dancers performing with a pop star at a stadium which I had choreographed. The pop star in question was Heather Small of M-People, and the kids were dancing with her to her 2 biggest hits 'Search For a Hero', and 'What Have You Done Today To Make You Feel Proud'. Unofficially, until accredited, we got the record, but it was a long and stressful day, so unfortunately you caught me right in the middle of it.)

REFLECTIONS ON ROSCOE

THE OLD ROSCOE PLACE METHODIST CHURCH was an intimidating building physically and spiritually, with its stained glass windows, particularly the large round one at the back of the church far up in the balcony that looked beautiful during the evening service when the sunset came through. There were stiff back pews and ancient worn cushions to kneel on, a powerful organ to rattle the roof, choir stalls and pulpit 10 feet off the ground behind a decorative and intricate communion rail. This was a Methodist 'high' church.

That church smelled wonderfully old— musky, damp, dusty— and as a child I was there every week for the morning service, back for the 2:00pm Sunday School, and if I was bored I would accompany my mum to the evening service on occasions for some personal exploration of those secret and hidden places. Only an eleven year old boy would relish this opportunity to play Indiana Jones for real!

I feel I must apologise to the members of Roscoe who may not be happy with much of what I will say but all these experiences have shaped the man I have become and I am grateful for every single one.

Prior to moving to the new church building in 1974 the old Sunday school was one of the most popular and well attended Sunday schools in the neighbourhood boasting a regular presence of 70-100 children and young people every week. The Christmas parties were organised chaos in its purest form with platefuls of potted beef sandwiches and strawberry jelly, Musical Chairs, Pass-the-Parcel and everybody's favourite 'the Hokey Kokey' when the boys would end up on the floor rolling about in dust and splinters in our Sunday best.

In my possession is a most important historical document that I jealously guard, handed to me by my favourite aunt and Sunday school teacher, Elsie Plumb. It is called *The Methodist Church Overseas Magazine* and has a black and white photograph of my sister Diana, with a good friend at the time, Carol Plumb, and myself staring at Miss Plumb. I never believed that our photo would end up being distributed around the planet! We were the first generation *(children of Caribbean parents)* born in this country and this magazine saw it as quite novel having these black faces in an English church. The presence of these young children saved the Sunday school and even expanded it.

I remember sitting at the front every week listening with rapt attention to all the biblical children's stories and learning the songs. Even today if I attend a conference I sit at the front to get the best seat. This room had an oil painting of a blond haired, blue-eyed, bearded Jesus surrounded by children from all over the planet, sitting on a rock with his arms and hands wide open. It's a comforting scene yet one that I would look at every week because it somehow disturbed me. As a three year old I didn't have the words to say what it was that troubled me but there was something not quite right with that painting. Maybe it was the half-naked African child reaching up from the floor; or could it have been that all the children were touching Jesus except the African child; even the European girl was sitting on his knee dressed in her Sunday best. It was not the obvious racism, it was something else more subtle. Occasionally I let my mind drift back to that room and look intently at that painting once again.

When reaching senior Sunday school at the start of our teenage years we sang non-Christian protest songs, for example 'If I had a hammer'

121

and songs by Bob Dylan and Johnny Cash. I really found this time in my life odd, yet very attractive because we were treated as young people. We had a new Sunday school teacher who was bringing up strange concepts such as the Vietnam War and politics; on more than a few occasions I wanted to go back to the comfort and safety of the Junior Sunday school. Unfortunately we were not allowed to do 'the Hokey Kokey' at the senior Sunday School Christmas parties but more grownup activities such as sitting around talking to each other. Junior Sunday School seemed more and more appealing.

However, I was given a chance to go back to Junior Sunday School as the pianist where I could play all the old familiar songs and tackle some new ones which I heartily enjoyed until the Church Stewards in the new Roscoe building changed the Sunday School time from a 1½ hour session at 2:00pm to a morning only gathering of less than 40 minutes. I still believe that was a tragic mistake where 80% of the children were lost and I still lament its passing.

Shortly before the old Roscoe was demolished, I stumbled into a room left open behind the organ. I discovered among the cobwebs some old music books and I quickly gathered the good ones together. Those old, torn organ books, with missing pages, were the foundation of the next stage of my personal development within the church.

A few months before the new Roscoe was opened I had one last chance to wander round the building site on a cold November Saturday morning, and I could not help feeling that I was hugely disappointed with the barn they were constructing. I knew immediately that the old Roscoe would be terribly missed and I would visit the demolition site before it was too dangerous to meander through the ruins. I still hold on to the memories of when I had to stand up in the old Roscoe main church to recite the 23rd psalm from memory, the countless wedding ceremonies and being severely told off for going near the organ— this was one area of the church the children were not allowed to venture into.

When the new Roscoe was opened, which could be easily turned into a hall for various activities, I remember being excited by the prospect of having a dual purpose building. Saturday nights were comedy nights for

122

talented young people and adults. This was in 1974 in Revd Trevor Bates' tenure. He must have had a vision for his young people because this is the time that the young people, particularly teenagers, flourished. We were given the chance to explore and experiment and the opportunity to discover practical Christianity through the Confirmation Classes.

At some point the Minister made the decision to train four young men, of which I was one, to play the organ. I was a reluctant recruit at first because I loved the piano; nevertheless this was a good chance to be part of a group of like-minded individuals and eventually becoming good friends. Organ lessons were given every Saturday morning for a few months and we had to travel across town to Oakwood. Towards the end of the first lesson the teacher asked me to sit and play a tune. The one I had been practising was 'the Can-Can' which I played with energy and enthusiasm. The organ teacher (Mr George Stoker) was appalled at my choice of music. It took me many years to understand what was so wrong with 'the Can-Can' on a church organ!

This 'gang of four' were loved by the Church members and our music skills were put to great use both within Roscoe and in other traditional churches, which we were happy to do. To me it was another opportunity to share the Christian faith. We even featured on the front page of the 'Yorkshire Evening Post', which made Roscoe very proud. Roscoe made funds available to send us further afield to gain more skills, knowledge and basically share our talents and remind everyone that the Methodist Church was now multi-cultural. One of these events was 'Youth Makes Music', a summer camp in Grantham for young Methodist musicians. We felt privileged to represent not only Roscoe but black young people in the country, even though we did not know it at the time.

At that time Roscoe seemed to be progressive and forward looking, but there were grumblings from the rigid members of the congregation. They would visit the youth club and harass the two youth workers Rod and Elaine, about its operations until the workers resigned from one of the best youth clubs in the area, and that sadly was the end of Roscoe Youth Club of about 100 members.

I was asked to join the Boys' Brigade as an officer which I really had no interest in but I was given the opportunity to run the Boys' Brigade football team for the Brigade by Captain Mr George Eubanks. There was no money to take them to matches, but despite this we managed to win the knock out cup in 1981 when we won 3 – 2. I actually learnt how to manage a team without knowing anything about people management but I proved inspirational enough to lead the team. For a short time we were able to restore the reputation and glory to the Roscoe 13th Boys' Brigade Company.

Saturday night comedy, drama and entertainment stemmed from my youthful arrogance and the ability to get other like-minded young people to all come together to perform silly sketches, sing songs, tell jokes and anything else we could think of, in front of a packed church. My two sisters, Diana and Heather, would form the backbone of all the acts. I could rely on them completely and I would take care of the technical aspects of running a show on the night. To my amazement each show worked fantastically well and inspired others to put on their own productions such as fashion and hair shows. For many years Roscoe Church on those Saturday nights was the only place to be in Chapeltown. It grew from the old Roscoe set in its gloomy lit Church with a couple of dozen members politely clapping a song or a recitation —to the crowded, raucous entertainment in a warm hybrid new Church hall.

It saddens me to reflect on how and why the Church failed to hang on to the youth that wanted to contribute so much. Only those rare individuals such as Elsie Plumb, Georgina Webbe and, in his own way, Trevor Bates were able to understand this. Georgina put up with so many of my antics with a smile and non-judgmental attitude which made her one of the few adults young people could approach.

Much of what I experienced growing up in Roscoe I was able to take with me when I left for London. Trevor Bates encouraged me to apply for the post of Youth Pastor at Harlesden Methodist Church in North West London. I had previously been on a Youth Exchange to the Cameroon and I was itching for more exciting episodes such as this outside of Leeds. He must have known that not only did I have all the abilities to fulfil that job in bucket loads, but that I might never come back to Roscoe.

I am truly grateful to Trevor Bates for pushing me forward for that job, I am not sure if he knew it at the time but he saved me. I had become disillusioned with my dead-end career and I could see all my hopes and dreams disappearing at only twenty five years of age. My spiritual life had stagnated and I couldn't see a way out until he handed me a small bit of paper which to my shame I didn't do anything about for a couple of weeks. I think I even missed the deadline.

I remember the words of Dr Pauline Webb, the former Vice President of the World Council of Churches, saying to me that I had a gift and calling to work with young people and she supported everything that I did with them. But the truth is it all comes back to Roscoe and its activities for the youth from the old church to the present and giving me time and space to nurture my talents. It's sad to see that this tradition hasn't been maintained. On my sporadic visits to the Church when I visit Leeds, it's nice to see the children in the morning but where are the teenagers? It's as if I am staring at that oil painting again in the old Sunday school room and me asking myself, "What is wrong with this picture?"

Stephen Woodley

REMINISCENCES OF MINISTERS AND DEACONESSES

REMINISCENCES OF ROSCOE
1972 – 1981
Revd Trevor S. Bates

IT IS HARD TO CONVEY to you the real sense of privilege and joy which Dorothy (my first wife) and I felt when we knew I was appointed to be a minister in the Leeds North East circuit in 1972. I was asked to take responsibility for Roscoe and Woodhouse Methodist Churches and have as a colleague the Revd Ian G. Lucraft, who was then in his first appointment as a probationer. We had returned that year from Belize having spent 18 years serving with the Methodist people in the Leeward Islands and in (Belize) British Honduras and the Republic of Honduras. We hoped and prayed that on our return to England we might be able to work with people from the Caribbean in this country. How fortunate we were!

We journeyed from Selly Oak, Birmingham, to the Leeds North East circuit at the end of August for the Circuit Welcome Service held at Chapel Allerton Methodist Church. Having returned from Central America early in August the Methodist Church Overseas Division required us to have three months leave before actually taking up circuit work in this country. So it wasn't until 1st December 1972 that we actually took up residence in the Manse at Gledhow Park Road and began getting to know the people, the churches of the section and the Inner City neighbourhoods of Leeds.

Ian Lucraft was with us for two years and then moved on to work with the Sheffield Inner City Ecumenical Team. Ian was followed by the Rev Raymond Garfoot, who remained one year before being moved to Middleton Methodist Church, South Leeds. Raymond was followed by two deaconesses— first, Sister Lily Dobbs who lived in Keighley and commuted to work with us for one year. Sister Lily was followed by Sister Margaret Horn who remained in the circuit after we left in 1981.

126

All were fine colleagues and brought commitment and enthusiasm into the circuit and to the section.

It was an exciting and demanding time to be involved with the building of two new churches— Woodhouse Methodist Church, which opened in August 1974, and of course, Roscoe Methodist Church, which opened in October 1974. The new start which each building offered to its people was grasped with both hands. Woodhouse was a newly combined congregation of Cambridge, Meanwood Road and Woodhouse Street, ready to play their full part in Christian witness — especially to the immediate community. Roscoe was by now, a predominantly West Indian congregation beginning to find its feet and becoming an exciting and unique church within the Leeds North East circuit.

One of the most exciting developments of the mid 70s was the willingness and the way West Indian members of the congregation took on responsibility for the complete management of the church's life. In this whole process we clearly saw how Caribbean people were 'standing tall' as new trust was put in them to handle the 'behind the scenes' jobs which were so important for Roscoe to run smoothly.

The story of different ventures is told elsewhere – the housing of the Chapeltown Citizen's Advice Bureau and of Roscoe Day Nursery in 1974, followed by the need for a West Indian Family Counselling Service to offer pastoral support and advice to people of the Caribbean community living in the neighbourhood. The demand for more space and facilities at Roscoe was also becoming painful! We found ourselves being driven to build again, so with generous help from the local authority, Willow House and Roscoe Hall were opened in 1981 to serve the wider community.

Within the life of the congregation – a pipe organ had been designed and installed for the new Roscoe, but finding organists became a challenge! However, God guided us to discover within our own congregation three and then a fourth West Indian youngster willing to be trained and learn to play that organ. Colin Robinson, Andrew Saddler, Stephen Woodley together with Mervyn Williams all became able organists for our worship, and we were proud of them!

When we arrived our son Andrew was still at Kingswood Methodist Boarding School at Bath, and when 15 years remained at home. Andrew did some further education in Leeds and then became an apprentice dental technician with a laboratory in Harrogate. He has remained a skilled dental technician ever since. It was also a time when Dorothy's mother died in July 1973 back in the West Indies and Dorothy returned to St Kitts for the funeral and the following family arrangements.

It was a great privilege to be involved in helping Okuro and Oyidiya Ndukwe to be married at Roscoe Place in 1973. Little did we know then what a future would unfold for them and their children. In 1980 they were accepted by our Methodist Church Overseas Division for service with the World Church in Nepal. It was a unique appointment, and Okuro served for five years before returning to live in Chapeltown to be with Roscoe again. Little did Okuro know that his daughter Nenna would take up an appointment as a clinical psychologist in Singapore in 2010!

To be invited to be one of two British representatives to the Conference of the MCCA in May 1979 held in Bridgetown, Barbados, was also a great privilege for me, more so because I was able to give some account of how people from the Leeward Islands were adjusting to life in Leeds! On 2nd March 1975 I was invited to do a Lenten Service on BBC Radio 4 when I was at Woodlands Methodist Church, Harrogate for their World Church Sunday. Then in March 1977 our Roscoe Sunday Morning Service was televised by Granada TV. The Revd Howard Smith, Sister Margaret Horn and myself, along with teenager Mervyn Williams as organist, with members of the congregation all participated.

The Methodist Conference decided in 1972 that all ministers should be responsible for their own furnishings in the manses and the transition year was 1972/73. Negotiations with the circuit stewards as we arrived in the circuit provided us with good quality basic furniture and the removal of items not to be kept. However, the circuit was also willing to purchase new beds for us! That really was luxury indeed and we were so grateful!

128

The Farewell events at both Woodhouse Methodist Church and Roscoe in the summer of 1981 became lasting memories for all of us. At Roscoe, in the new Sports Hall, the Farewell Dinner with its sumptuous menu, a 'This Is Your Life' surprise presentation and the gift of a Sun-Burst Clock (which is still working to this day!) and the many speeches of good wishes – rounded off our years in the Leeds North East circuit as being unique for us.

We moved on to the Pudsey & Farsley Circuit in August 1981. However the memories, the friendships and the blessings of having shared in the life of both Roscoe and Woodhouse Methodist congregations in those years of considerable change have remained with us across the years. Our lives were permanently enriched, and for that we praise the Lord.

PS I would like to place on record that for Dorothy, the nine years with Leeward Islands people in Leeds and at Roscoe, were some of the most precious years of her life – not least because she was a Kittian herself and felt very much at home among you during our stay.

ROSCOE
Revd Gerald Bostock

I WAS A PROBATIONER MINISTER at Roscoe for two years, from 1965 to 1967. It was a memorable experience, and a happy one. One of the things I most readily recall, at this long distance in time, was the Order of Morning Prayer Service, which we held every month. This was always a very well attended service with everyone coming in their Sunday best and in high spirits. People sang the canticles and the responses, which they knew by heart, with great gusto. Since then, I have always been convinced that a simple but popular liturgy is a great aid to worship and the celebration of the gospel. On one occasion the Order of Morning Prayer Service was on television. I took part in the service. It was somewhat nerve-racking, but all went well and it helped to put Roscoe on the map.

Another thing that stands out in my mind was the Anglo-West Indian Fellowship which flourished at that time and was a great source of renewal and friendship. I also remember the Community Lunch, which

129

was attended by the local MP and by various community leaders; this was organised by Malcolm Furness, and by Mary Stratton, the General Secretary of the Leeds Council of Social Service who brought along with her one of her young social workers, Pamela Ashdown, whom I married shortly after leaving Roscoe in the summer of 1967— one particular good reason for remembering Roscoe! So Roscoe does indeed bring back some happy memories, and it is good to know that the stream of faith and love which was flowing then is flowing still.

Blessings on you all
Gerald (and Pam) Bostock

MEMORIES OF ROSCOE
Sister Stella Bullivant

LOOKING AT PHOTOGRAPHS of my time at Roscoe has brought back so many memories.

Children enjoying the Summer Play School, babies being baptized, the Sunday School, the Boys' Brigade and Girls' Brigade, Youth Club, all tell of the great care for young people The ladies in the kitchen, always busy, always much laughter. The Luncheon Group, The Womens Meeting, the outings.

The care for others, in the church and in the local community as Mary (Saddler) was there for all. The Laundrette to answer a need in the area. The involvement with the CAB and Nursery meeting on Roscoe premises, the Sunday worship , the singing and choir, all very specially Roscoe.

Of course I remember the people mostly, some now passed on, others grown up now and in their turn being Roscoe in Chapeltown.

It was for me a great privilege to be part of Roscoe in that special, unique part of Leeds.

God bless,
Stella

130

A FEW REMINISCENCES OF ROSCOE
Revd Michael J. Chapman

IT WAS JUNE 1970 and I had been a minister in the Yeovil Circuit in Somerset for two years. The Chairman of the Southampton District telephoned me to tell me that the Stationing Committee was pulling me out of Yeovil to go to a priority appointment in Leeds. We came up to Chapel Allerton and met the Superintendent, the Revd W.N. Stainer Smith, and he took us to see Malcolm Furness, the Minister for Roscoe. Malcolm was to take me to see Roscoe, but he would not take my wife, Sheila, nor my children Mary and Dawn. He was probably afraid that if they saw the church they would refuse to come.

The Victorian building of the church stood alone amongst the rubble of the demolished housing around it. At that time there were no plans to rebuild. I agreed to come on the understanding from the Chairman of the Leeds District that although my initial invitation was for three years I would not be moved again for more years than that.

At that time Roscoe still had Morning Prayer one Sunday a month, so one of my first duties was to go down to the church and meet the organist and learn to sing the versicles – 'O Lord open thou our lips', etc. It was a new experience but I enjoyed it at first as the Service ran itself without me having to think. But then one of my girls noticed that in one of the collects we addressed God as 'lover of concord.' It was about the time that Concorde was beginning to fly and after that I had a job not to giggle as I said that prayer.

One of our biggest problems was that as there were no people living near the church we had break-ins almost every Saturday night. It was not unusual to go on a Sunday morning and find the vestry floor covered with insulation material where thieves had tried to break into the safe. The only things in the safe were the Marriage Registers so they would have been disappointed if they had succeeded. Surely it does not take a lot of intelligence to know that it is unlikely that there would be anything in a church safe on a Saturday night – Sunday night might be different!

I had been at Roscoe for only 18 months when I was told that my invitation was not being extended. I would have to leave after my three years. As Sheila was at teacher training college and the girls were in the middle of 'O' Level and 'A' Level courses I decided that I could not move so easily. I resigned after two years and went to the James Graham teacher training college and took my Teaching Certificate. I taught at Braim Wood and then St Matthew's Middle Schools and then returned to the Stations in 1984 and went to Haworth in the Keighley Circuit, then as Super to the Farnworth Circuit in Bolton. Sheila died in 1996 and I retired in 1997 and came back here to Keighley. I still preach on alternate Sundays and take my share of funeral services.

People who remember me will probably remember my ministry as the short interlude between the longer stays of Malcolm Furness and Trevor Bates.

MEMORIES OF ROSCOE
Revd Robert B. Creamer
1992 – 2006

I HAD A GOOD FEELING, and a tremendous sense of excitement to be minister of Roscoe Methodist Church, and I was not disappointed. My family and I were warmly welcomed by members, and by Sister Eileen Gaunt, the deaconess. This togetherness and warmth continued throughout my fourteen years at Roscoe.

The last weekend in August is the West Indian Carnival, and as a family we attended the Sunday morning service at Roscoe. As I entered the building, I was asked if I can play the piano, as the organist had not arrived! (I can play the piano, but only for my own listening). The shortage of organists had remained a difficulty throughout the circuit.

The congregation stands as the choir enters the church singing a chorus, followed by the preacher. My concern for the choir remained, and even though they tried to do their best, they were unable to maintain a regular number of choir members, they did not have a choir master, nor adequate Choir practice. However, they progressed to getting themselves choir gowns.

One of my first ambitions at Roscoe was to get headed notepaper for the Church. I felt that this was professionally correct, even considering the cost at the time.

After years of use, the plastic chairs in the Church were showing their age. They were collapsing when in use, and so we had no choice but to replace them. We chose wooden padded chairs at a cost of £8,000. Within a short time of fundraising and donations, we had sturdy comfortable chairs which matched the carpet.

We progressed to buying bibles for the Church, including for the Sunday School children – a bible for each chair. Members paid for bibles which they donated in remembrance of a relative or friend, or as a gift to the Church. There was also a general donation, and our ambition was fulfilled. We also bought new hymn books—*Hymns and Psalms*, and *Complete Mission Praise*.

One of my concerns at Roscoe was the refusal of members to take on specific duties for the running of the Church. I had to outline the structure of the Church committees and explain responsibilities which we all have to ensure the continued life of the Church. I continued to persuade, encourage, guide, and manage those who were reluctant, in order to increase their self-confidence. Gradually volunteers came forward.

The Girls' and Boys' Brigades, and the Roscoe Steel Band had problems of non-attendance of members, and also of leaders of these groups.

New people were received into membership of the Church every year, and baptisms were also frequent. Unfortunately the parents did not return to Church after their children were baptised, despite various efforts to encourage them back. For Mothering Sunday, Father's Day and Christmas services, they were sent special invitations which some of them accepted.

The Sunday School Christmas musicals were very good. One year they performed the African Christmas using the suitable props. The children gave hours of their time to practise, and performed with enthusiasm. It was a great success.

I was proud of the way the premises were used for the benefit of the community – Citizens Advice Bureau, Day Nursery, and for social and business needs by other groups in the community, and also as host to congregations from other parts of the world.

Getting to know one another within the Church had to be encouraged, and our efforts were successful to a large extent.

I was always interested in the timing members had when they attended the services. During the singing of the second hymn, several people would be walking in, so that by the end of that hymn there were more people in Church than at the beginning of the Service. Why?

It was satisfying to have ministerial students. I am happy to say that one of my students, Graeme Dutton, was ordained on August 15, 2010, and is a minister in the Leeds NE circuit.

My experience of West Indian funerals was a learning one. Families were involved in every aspect of the funeral arrangements, and their love and care for the deceased and for one another were very obvious. Also the support people gave to other bereaved families even when they did not know one another.

Eventually in 1997 we started a Bereavement Support Group at Roscoe, to provide direct contact with families within the community, regardless of which Church they attended or none. We held a yearly Remembrance Service, and not only invited those with whom we were in contact, but there was an open invitation to everyone else. These services were well attended. Also we held a seminar every year with an invited speaker on the subject of bereavement.

The financial challenges of Roscoe were ongoing. For example, the rental reviews with CAB and Roscoe Day Nursery, keeping WIFCOS and the Luncheon Club project afloat, and the repair and maintenance of the entire building. When the Quinquennial Report highlighted that Roscoe's roof needed replacing, we realised that it would be an

134

expensive undertaking, and eventually started fundraising. With all these ongoing problems, I was very hesitant to open a letter addressed to me from a legal firm. Some days later when I plucked up courage and opened it, I read that Dorothy Ramsden, one of our long-standing members had bequeathed £10,000 to Roscoe. Phew!! What a joyous relief!

A new poster board, new notice board, and landscaping part of the garden, gave a new and fresh look to Roscoe. We also had a Welcome notice at the entrance of the Church. This was given to Roscoe free of charge by the gardener/joiner. We achieved these with the help of a full grant from Leeds City Council of £500. The total cost was £2,637.87.

The arguments which went on during the Finance/Property meetings were incredible. For instance, why was £2.50 spent to buy a bucket, when it could have been bought for £1.50!

I introduced an "Open Service" on the second Sunday evening in each month. This was to encourage members to express their personal thoughts, happy or sad, or their general observations of life. The congregation could then share in whatever choice of hymn, bible reading or prayers which individuals felt would help them in their daily life.

My first Sabbatical at Roscoe was quite an experience. I was invited and encouraged by members to visit the Caribbean islands of St Kitts and Nevis, from where a large number of members came. I was overwhelmed by the sense of love and understanding of members of the congregation, when a substantial financial donation was given to me for the visit. Alberta (daughter of George & Pearline Freeman who were members of Roscoe, and had returned to Nevis to live) arranged for me to stay with her parents in Nevis. I also spent some time with the local minister in St Kitts, the Revd Charles Seaton. They also gave me a list of their friends and relatives to visit. From my date of arrival up to the time I left the airport, I was well taken care of. I have very happy memories of my visit.

Another joyous time was when I celebrated my 50th birthday. I am still using the bread-making machine which was a gift from the Church. I

135

have a montage of photographs of Roscoe members, and also of my visit to St Kitts and Nevis. Also a specially framed 3D photograph of Roscoe Church on display.

The love and care expressed to me in so many ways by the members of Roscoe Methodist Church, remain in the forefront of my memories.

THE HISTORICAL JOURNEY OF ROSCOE METHODIST CHURCH
Revd J. Malcolm Furness (1927-2005)
Roscoe 1962–70

LOOKING BACK OVER OUR DIARIES for the eight happy years at Roscoe we can see what an exciting time it was for us personally and for the Church. Both our children were born in Leeds, Julie only a month after our arrival, and Robert in 1964. In the midst of the 1963 snow, we moved manse from Oak Road to Gledhow Park Road, where we couldn't explore the garden until the thaw a month later!

The Church we came to was a busy, vibrant community where something was happening every day— BB, Youth Club, Church Fellowship, Vestry Hour, Women's Fellowship, and the Sunday congregation was a healthy mixture of white, black and brown— West Indian, African and natives. Later we welcomed a Cypriot, an Hungarian and an Indian doctor to our multiracial flock. Roscoe was busy – three weddings on our first Saturday, four baptisms on the first Sunday. But that was nothing, twice in our time we had 13 baptisms in one service, and once we christened five babies on TV.

As we look back, we remember all those now dead, who were stalwarts of the Roscoe work, West Indians re-starting their Methodist Church life after coming from St Kitts and Nevis, and people born in the church who had welcomed newcomers with open arms. The Church which had been the birthplace of the Wesley Guild (1890s) was ready for the social changes taking place.

It was a good time to be alive, and all was exciting, but of course, some things stand out. In 1964 we had a big Stewardship campaign that

136

revolutionised the church's finances and made us all think again of our obligations in time and talents. In September 1965 Gerald Bostock joined us as the first of three fine Probationer Ministers. Two years later, Gerald was replaced by Kenneth Glendinning who sadly died in his middle ministry and in 1969 by Peter Williamson. All were good, able and willing colleagues with much to offer.

There were two memorable Anglo-West Indian group holidays, the first to Ilkley when we stayed at the Deaconess College, the second at Cliff College, Derbyshire, when everybody enjoyed themselves in lovely summer weather.

1967 was an outstanding year even by Roscoe standards. That Summer, we had the help of a group of lively Winant Volunteers, students from America who taught us how to handle frisbees, and (with local volunteers) helped us run the first large scale Holiday Play Scheme in Leeds – probably the first in the country. On the first morning we had a queue of boys and girls waiting at 8.30, and we ran all the month of August with a mixed programme of indoor and outdoor activities, a pattern for what later became national holiday schemes. That was a great success, and one of which Roscoe can be justly proud.

Emancipation day was always celebrated, but in August 1966, our service was televised live by the BBC. Five babies were baptised in front of a nationwide audience, and the much loved Parson (*Revd William*) Sunter gave the blessing. In December 1969 we were on TV. Again for an hour – this time a children's Christmas Celebration on the ITV Network. We involved children from all the local schools, and proudly showed our Yorkshire origin by singing 'While Shepherds' to the tune of Ilkley Moor baht hat! That programme was recorded on Thursday evening and broadcast to Britain and Ireland on Sunday 21st December.

What a time it was! We remember the busy Working Lunches of local social workers, the beginnings of the Studley Grange Children's Organisation, the Aggrey Housing Society, and all the local movements in which Roscoe had its part. It was a good time for which we are grateful, and we send greetings from all of us for the future of all of you.   ***Margery, Malcolm, Julie and Robert (Furness)***

RECALLING ROSCOE DAYS
(1976–82 with Revd Trevor Bates and Revd John Whittle)

Sister Margaret (Deaconess Margaret Horn)

WHAT A CONTRAST as I moved from village life in Durham to live and work in the Inner-city! I had to learn quickly how to be streetwise —especially when the police called on me to say that they believed my car had been involved with the 'Ripper Case'. They soon realised that this was not so.

I discovered some of the West Indian way of life and admired the fortitude and courage of those who came over to cope with England and join in worship that must have been cold in more ways than one.

Fortunately, some of the church members did give a welcome and hospitality, causing the church to meet present needs.

My memories are of a church that was developing and mostly West Indian. The Sunday school was large and there was a good group of teenagers. Three of the teenagers became our organists and served in a remarkable way – due to the foresight of an older man who had served the church in that capacity for many years.

Each year, I was expected to organise a Holiday Play Scheme and I still have the notes from the last one. I've had exceptionally good leaders and lively teenagers' help. It was impossible to limit the age group as whole families came together. Our trips to local and wider areas were happy and the discipline of the children on local and private buses was good – though they would let off steam when in the building at Roscoe.

It is good to know that the church is progressing in such an area of Leeds.

May God richly bless you.

138

ROSCOE PLACE LEEDS
West Indian work 1954 onwards

Revd J. Russell Moston
(Extracts from a diary kept by Russell whilst a student at Wesley College, Headingley, Leeds)

"The Revd Harry Salmon was the minister of Roscoe Place, Chapeltown Leeds in 1954. He noted that several West Indians were 'settling' in the area and felt that the church had a responsibility to care for them. He soon discovered that help was required if the work was to be continued. He invited the College to make the work known amongst the students, to see if anyone would like to help. I offered myself to see if I was a suitable 'candidate'."

"**Sat/20/Nov/1954** – Revd Harry Salmon gave me a list of folk to visit. Caught tram to Harehills Avenue – *(or so I thought!* it was a filthy night, and afterwards I found that I had gone to the wrong street!) However, I knocked on a door several times, having seen someone in the hallway, but no one came. Just as I was turning to leave, two white men came up the path. I asked if this was number 12, Harehills Avenue. They said "yes", thus confirming my mistaken idea! They both knocked, with the same result. Then one of them opened the door, and we all three went into the hallway. I knocked at the nearest door, but still no one in sight. The white men said they were looking for somewhere to stay, so I gave them one of the addresses I had, telling them to be prepared to find coloured folk there. We then went our separate ways."

"I made my way through the thick fog to Harry's Manse (3 Oak Road). I wanted to double check the other addresses. Harry and Greta invited me in for supper after my visits. At every place I called at (5 in all), the people I wanted to see were out. This gave me an insight into what to expect in my work! A sense of fear; filth and indifference seemed to be everywhere."

"One house in particular stands out. When I knocked on the door (I had a long wait, as I was now becoming accustomed to doing!), the door was unlocked, unbolted and unbarred, then a coloured man said 'Well,

139

what d'yar want?' I asked to see a Mr Thomas Scrocope. He said he would see if there was anyone of that name, and shut the door in my face. I waited and prayed silently. He eventually came back, and said, (jerking his head in invitation), 'Come in.' I went in! He took me to a room about as big as our 'Dens' (*study rooms at College*). The atmosphere was so hot that my glasses steamed up! I took them off, and nearly fell down a step I failed to see. I peered through the thick fog of tobacco smoke, and saw, sitting round a little table in one corner of the room, five men, a young woman, and a child of about 4 years (all coloured). The men were playing dominoes ...

"A rough looking man said, 'Huh, they's two fellows not one – a Mr Thomas and a Mr Procope. Take him to Mr Thomas,' he said to the man who had let me in ... I was taken up the stairs, clouds of dust coming from the moth-eaten carpet under our feet. The place was filthy and reeked terribly. He called 'Thomas' all the way up the stairs in a solemn, dead voice. The bedroom doors were all painted in a bright vivid red, and had catches on the *outside*! A man came out of a room, which was in complete darkness, and I once again explained what I wanted. He seemed a well dressed man, and educated; in fact he looked out of place in the surroundings. He looked into another bedroom, and then said, 'Sorry Sir, but they are not in.'

"I reported my failures and adventures to Harry. Had supper and made my way back to College. I climbed in through the window about 11.15pm very tired and very humble. I suddenly realised (in an infinitely inferior way) what our Lord must have felt – to offer love, and friendship, and to have it misunderstood, and even openly rejected. I prayed hard ... I knew how much I needed God if I was to do anything at all!

"Sunday 21st/Nov: My next port of call was the house I described earlier. This time an Irish lad, aged about 18 years opened the door. He asked me in, and took me to the same little room that I went to last night. Again, I had to remove my glasses because of the heat. He tapped one of the coloured men on the shoulder and said, 'This is Mr Procope.' I asked Mr Procope if I could have a word with him ... took me to his bedroom ... no better than the rest of the house ... poorly furnished ... wireless blaring. He told me his father was the Editor of

140

the St Kitts daily Bulletin, and produced a copy to prove it. He said he was a Methodist, but wanted to settle in the country before he found a church ... I told him about Roscoe Place, and invited him to come along ... He promised he would come.

"I then walked to the Manse and reported my afternoon's work to Harry over tea. After tea Greta and I went to Roscoe Place, and it did my heart good to see that Procope had turned up with another man named Poole! There were *eight* coloured people present in the Service. We started with *two!* A Student Deaconess was preaching, and she did very well indeed. Bryan Ewin also attended the service, and we went back with the Deaconess as far as City Square, where she left us to catch the 'bus back to Ilkley College.

"Sun (Sat?)/4th/Dec: After tea, put 'collar' on and caught Tram to Chapeltown. Called on a Mr Z. Lewis who was still in bed. Prayed with him. Went on the see Frank G. Frances and Victor Harris. Went through the Membership lessons with them.

"Sun/5th/Dec: Bryan Ewin and I caught the Tram to Chapeltown, intending to visit all the contacts with the coloured people, but when we called on the first one, Mr John Griffiths, we stayed for about an hour!...because we met Mr Eldermeier Fairclough and a Mr Crawford. Mr Crawford asked 'What Church are you from, Reverend?' I said 'Methodist, where do you attend?' 'Well, Reverend I goes no place.' 'O well, I think we can do something for you.' ... After much conversation, I led in prayer.

"1955: Sat/Jan 15th: At night, visited Frank and Victor. Took them through another lesson for Membership. Spoke to Harry regarding the possibility of having a room at Roscoe Place for a West Indian Service on a Saturday Night.

"Tue/Feb/1st: Delivered letter to all known W.I's about the service on a Saturday Night at 8pm. Attended meeting of the Aggrey Soc. I was distressed that the Committee discussed more about socials, dancing and suppers etc. rather than work, accommodation and colour prejudice.

141

"Sat/Feb/5th: 7.30pm West Indian Service – **17 present!** ... no one to play the piano, and no one with a guitar – so I had to start the Hymns off. We had testimonies, and Mr Lewis called the Meeting to prayer. Plenty of 'Amen' and Hallelujah'. We had Roman Catholic, Moravian, a member of the Church of God, and two people who were already Methodists, and want to transfer their Membership.'

"Sat/Feb/19th: Had 11 W.Indians at Fellowship, which went very well indeed.

"Sun/Feb/20th: Took evening service at Roscoe. 15 W.Indians present. The largest number present on a Sunday so far.

"Sun/Nov/13th: Went to Roscoe. There were **210 W.Indians at the service**. At the fellowship we had about 100 W.Indians, and a good number of English people! |We sang with gusto, many of the old Hymns and choruses.

"1958: Sept. 3rd: Moved back to Leeds from Manchester – after Ordination, and Marriage to Hilda, as minister ... a quick look at my diaries did not reveal much information ... one or two memories to give a 'flavour'.

"When I first arrived back, we had a growing number of Weddings, but each time they were very late. I sometimes had as many as four on a Saturday, and each one was late, it caused great problems! I worked out a system, which meant that 99% were on time. The local vicar asked me the secret, and I said I would tell him when the time came for us to leave Leeds. I told each couple (most of whom had been living together for some time), what the total fees were, and that if they were on time, they would receive half of the fees back again. It seemed to work, and I was strict enough to charge the full fee if they were late – news travelled fast!

"The first Sunday in August was always a packed Church, including the gallery, because this was *Freedom Sunday*. I wish I could convey the sight! The Church looked like a bouquet of flowers, with so many bright *(glaring)* colours worn by both women and girls (and some of the men!)"

142

MARKED TURNING POINT IN THE LONG HISTORY OF ROSCOE PLACE
Revd Harry Salmon 1954 – 1958

CONGREGATIONS IN THE VERY LARGE church on my first Sunday were very small. What was unusual for those days, however, was the presence of black faces as well as white faces in both the morning and evening congregations. There were two Boys' Brigade members from Jamaica who were attending an international gathering with which Roscoe's own fine BB Company were involved. There was also a West Indian couple who also attended the evening service and returned with us to the manse for coffee. We enjoyed a conversation in which our knowledge of both the islands of St Kitts and Nevis and their population was greatly improved. At a personal level it also greatly influenced the course of our ministry and enabled me to see a way forward for Roscoe.

Mr and Mrs Lewis gave me addresses of recent arrivals from the West Indies. With the help of students from the Headingley College under the leadership of Russell Moston, we visited these multi-occupied houses to welcome the new arrivals, offer support and invite them to Roscoe. We also became acutely aware of the hardships suffered during the early months of living in this country. Exploitation of immigrants was rife, racial prejudice was often encountered and only the least desirable jobs were available.

Most of the people moving into Chapeltown came from two small islands – St Kitts and Nevis.

A year later, there was another event which helped to give Roscoe a new lease of life. Lincoln Fields, a small inner-city Methodist Church closed. Most of its few members chose to come to Roscoe and in spite of their own sense of loss, they enthusiastically participated in the life of the new church. Just when it seemed as though Roscoe's best days were in the past, these two developments gave it a new lease of life.

In 1954 Roscoe became like many large inner-city churches. Congregations had moved out into ever expanding suburbs. However, the splendid church officers who lived a bus or car journey away, returned to the church in order to support the opportunities presented by the arrival of fellow Christians from the Caribbean.

The old Roscoe with St Clement's Parish Church were situated on opposite sides of Chapeltown Road. Synagogues, rather than churches, were a feature of the area, though increasingly members of the Jewish community had moved out to Chapel Allerton and beyond. In the mid-fifties there were few links between different racial and cultural groups, but Chapeltown offered a non-threatening environment. Beneath the surface, however, there was exploitation and prejudice.

In Winter, often the only way of providing warmth was by using calor gas and paraffin heaters. Our climate provided a sharp contrast to the sun and warmth of the Caribbean and the need for warm clothing imposed an additional burden on what were unusually low incomes.

Our list of addresses was growing and through our visiting we became familiar with the kind of problem faced by people settling in a country with a hostile climate and an entirely different environment. Roscoe became widely known for the work we were doing at both a pastoral and social level. As minister I became involved in the wider responses to immigration. A solicitor in Leeds formed the Aggrey Society which had a short but useful life. Dr Aggrey had argued that just as we need the black and white keys of a piano, so we need the black and white people living and working in harmony. This simple analogy resonated with us at Roscoe and was a message we tried to get across in the numerous talks we were asked to give in Leeds and beyond.

There were pedlars of encyclopaedias and insurance policies who pursued the immigrants to purchase books that would help them and their children to get on in this country. Failure to keep up with the payment arrangement resulted in threatening legal action. A public house on Camp road announced a colour bar, and again we took up the issue.

In many ways, the life of Roscoe was enriched by the presence of vibrant enthusiastic Christians. The quality of our hymn singing improved and began to match the quality of the organ music. Baptisms became a feature of morning services and often on a Saturday we

144

would have several weddings whereas in the past they had been increasingly rare events; but the churches presented a culture shock to the new arrivals. They were amazed at how old and empty our large churches were. They also missed the more formal service of Morning Prayer that had been a feature of churches at home.

The atmosphere was warm, the singing was a delight and the fellowship was rich. Whenever there was a memorable anniversary linked to the history of the West Indies, we planned an evening service around it and on these occasions, white people experienced a little of what it must feel to belong to a minority group.

Greta and I had four exciting years at Roscoe Place. I was learning as I went along. My theological college training had done nothing to equip me for work in an inner-city church located in a cosmopolitan part of a large city. For both us Leeds was an enriching experience. Peter our only child was born in Leeds and for a short period he and his wife returned. During that period, we visited the new Roscoe and briefly experienced the warmth of the church community. It was a joy to see people with a Caribbean background sustaining the church.

We could never forget Leeds even if we wanted.

ROSCOE PLACE 1946 – 1952
Doreen Warman (daughter of Revd Lewis H. Allison)

WE ARRIVED IN SEPTEMBER 1946, when I was 12 years old along with my elder sister Jean and younger sister Christine. John (now (2010) superintendent minister Colchester circuit) was born in 1948.

My father, the Revd Lewis H Allison, came to Leeds Brunswick Circuit as the minister of Roscoe Place, Thorner and Seacroft, after surviving a horrendous train accident at Durham in January that year, at the time when the Revd Lawson Jones followed the Revd Leslie Weatherhead as superintendent minister.

It was the immediate post war era. During the war the churches had been denuded of their menfolk—families had been split by evacuation,

145

and relatives in different parts of the country were looking after their children. The churches were beginning to pick up. The Methodist Church was foremost at this time with a mission to reach young people, with its strong and inspiring leadership from the Methodist Youth Department.

Roscoe at this time was certainly a lively church, full of activity. There was a strong Boys' Brigade. The 13th Leeds BB was a legend in the area. It had a good, strong leadership team of totally committed leaders, some of whom were church stewards. Names I remember are Frank Farrar, who was also Sunday School Superintendent, Mr *(Tom)* Boyle and Colonel ? *(J R Simpson)*. On monthly Parade Sundays the brigade paraded round the streets led by its band, always drawing crowds to listen to the band, and watch the mace bearer spectacularly throw up and miraculously catch the mace! There was also the junior branch of Life Boys for which there was always a waiting list of local lads wishing to join.

Girl Guiding was well represented by Brownies and Guides. The Brownies were led by Brown Owl Eileen Gaunt, who was also a wonderful Christian lady. She was a night nurse, who opted to do permanent night duties, in order to look after her ailing parents. She ran a lovely pack and would regularly write little rhyming plays for the Brownies to perform at various church functions.

Eileen always felt the call to the mission field. But it wasn't until her parents had died that she felt free to follow that call, which she did by first training as a Deaconess at the Ilkley College. She was eventually appointed to the mission field in the West Indies.

I was a member of the Girl Guides, where we had a great time under the leadership of our captain, Joyce Reyner, who was also District Commissioner at the time – inspiring us to our full potential in Guiding, enabling us to go camping with the District Guides. Rangers were later started by Doris Lythe, another wonderful lady. She also started up, together with a young man recently demobbed from the army, the Young People's Discussion Group, which studied the Bible in depth. This was to become the basis for a membership group, and a Youth Mission team taking services round the circuit.

The Sunday School was a large one, with Beginners, Primary, Junior and Senior Departments. When I was 14 the SS Superintendent asked a group of us to become teachers in the large Primary department. We had weekly training classes, and a group of us went to the Methodist Youth Department Summer Schools for SS teachers at Shrewsbury and Bangor, N Wales.

My father was passionate about youth work and caring for the elderly. He started a youth club, which readily took off with members of the BB and Guiding amongst the first to join. I remember seeing the large hall full of young people. Table tennis, snooker, darts, arts and crafts, and learning ballroom dancing, were among some of the activities. A group of us joined with others from the Circuit to attend some of the early MAYC London Weekends. A great adventure, going down by coach and sleeping in the London Underground on bunk beds. Attending Methodist Central Hall and services at Wesley's Chapel, and 5000 of us filling the Royal Albert Hall for the final meeting.

We also attended Methodist Youth Camps held each year at Harlech meeting with young people from all over Britain. Another memorable occasion was when the Revd Len Barnett, General Secretary for youth work at MYD, came to lead a weekend at our club.

There was a strong lay leadership of both men and women. (*In Roscoe Place Church*) Among names I remember are Arthur and Elsie Firth, Frank Farrar and his wife, the Boyle family, Mabel Tate, Miss Vickers (the Beginner's leader), the Ackroyd family, especially Elsie and Gladys.

There was always strong support for Overseas Missions. For me the Circuit OM Week was a highlight, when four missionaries would arrive on Saturday to be introduced and spend the rest of the week taking services and meetings around the Circuit. It was through these that I had a call to OM work in the future.

This was a time when Overseas Missions was a great feature of Church life (e.g. Eileen Gaunt). When my husband went to the Gold Coast in 1955 he was one of 600 missionaries serving overseas, in China, India, Burma, Africa and the West Indies. That year he was one of 100

147

missionaries returning to the field at the farewell service at the Methodist Central Hall in London.

It was the arrival at church one morning of two West African students from the Gold Coast, later to become Ghana, that was to change the course of the life of Roscoe Place. I think it was 1947 when Dan Brown and Quafo Manti joined Roscoe. It was unusual then to see coloured people. They received a warm welcome, church members took them to heart and welcomed them into their homes. I was to meet them both later in 1960 when I went to Ghana. Dan Brown had become General manager of the 1,000 Ghana Government Schools, and Quafo Manti was now a doctor.

On one occasion, coming home from school, I found them both at home in the Manse in Oak Road. They had been turned out of their digs because they had chicken pox! They were nursed by our mother, and stayed with us for several weeks until they found new lodgings. (meanwhile Christine caught chicken pox!) From them I learned so much about Ghana – and Quafo said "You must come to the Gold Coast." Which I did in 1960 when I married Noel (*Warman*) in Accra.

These years were an exciting time in the life of the Church. Roscoe Place was alive with the Gospel and a sense of mission. It was also a time when I personally came to know Christ, along with ten or twelve of my friends.

MEMORIES OF ROSCOE
Revd David Whitehall

MANDY AND I CAME TO ROSCOE IN 1987. We were sent by the Methodist Conference as the church had been without a minister for two years.

During our time at Roscoe we set up a Youth Group that met at the Manse. Perhaps the highlight of the youth work while we were there was the time when the young people, along with others from the circuit, went to the MAYC Weekend in London and put on a presentation at the Royal Albert Hall about Steve Biko, the South African anti-apartheid activist who died in police custody, based on the film "Cry Freedom."

Soon after we arrived I started a midweek Bible Study and Prayer Group. We had some really good meetings and discussions and, over five years, some people said God had really helped them grow spiritually through those meetings.

I also introduced the idea of a monthly service of prayers for healing. On at least two occasions we felt God was very close to us during those services and I remember people becoming very moved and crying quietly at the communion rail.

In 1991 we went to visit some friends who were working on the island of St Martin in the Caribbean and this enabled us to fly the short distance to St Kitts and Nevis and see many of the places that people at Roscoe had told us about.

Perhaps the strongest memory I have is of the big special occasions like Easter Sunday when the church would be packed out with people - expectant, rejoicing and colourfully dressed for the big day.

ROSCOE ORGANISATIONS

THE LEEDS 27th GIRLS' BRIGADE COMPANY
My Reflections
Myrna Tyrell

I HAD BEEN A MEMBER of the GB (Girls' Brigade) Company in Nevis, West Indies, and became a Warrant Officer. When Girls' Brigade was introduced to Roscoe by the then minister the Revd Trevor Bates in 1975, I gladly offered to become an officer of the 27th Leeds Company. Within a short time the membership grew to 40 girls in the 5–14+ years age range.

The Captain was the late Elsie Plumb, who was very devout. The officers were Mary Saddler, Georgina Webbe, Dorothy Lunn, Louise Crumbie and myself.

Girls' Brigade is a spiritual and regimental organisation. With God's help our aim was to provide the mental and moral training of the Girls and help them to become self-confident and with a Christian attitude. One of these girls, now an adult, was happy to recall her years as a member of the GB to me.

I don't remember the exact date when I became Captain of the Company, but it was during 1990 that I gave up being an officer. I feel privileged to have been the first appointed black Captain in Leeds and possibly in West Yorkshire.

It was a delight to take the Company to parade services and functions. One event which I will never forget, took place at York Minster. The 27th Company played the Stevie Wonder song, "I just Called To Say I Love You". It was played on the Steel Band. The applause was resounding and we all felt very proud of their achievement.

The 27th Leeds Company continues to function.

MR LESLIE W. FARNILL - A Tribute

There can be few Methodist churches that have been better or longer served by an organist than was Roscoe Place by Leslie Farnill. As one who enjoyed his loyalty and support for eight years, I venture to pay tribute to his work on the organ he loved so much and played so professionally.

For forty–seven years he delighted the Roscoe membership by his sensitive accompaniment of congregational singing and his well-chosen and expertly performed incidental music. Possessed of a singularly fine instrument, our church was fortunate indeed to have at the console an accomplished musician who could bring out its tonal qualities to the full. On two occasions (the first of them when Leslie was already 75 years old) a nation-wide audience saw and heard his music in TV services. The letters of appreciation that followed were only a fitting tribute to the skill with which he grasped the possibilities and coped with the limitation of television broadcasting.

A man of many parts, Leslie Farnill also served his church as first Editor of *NEWS and VIEWS*, and his expert handling of copy and immense skill in payout and proofing allowed us to enjoy a church newsletter that was a model of what such publications should be.

Wise, capable, adaptable and friendly, Leslie Farnill was the best of colleagues. No tribute can be adequate, but all who worked with him and were privileged to enjoy his friendship will be grateful for all that he did, for all that he was, and for the example of long-continued, thoroughly dependable and completely self-effacing service that he left for us to follow.

Malcolm Furness

ROSCOE METHODIST CHURCH CHOIR

The present Roscoe Methodist Church building was opened on October 5th 1974. Amongst its congregation were four boys —Andrew Saddler, Stephen Woodley, Mervyn Williams and Colin Robinson—who were taught by the organist Mr Farnill to play the organ. The assistant organist Mr Stoker was also helpful.

Andrew Saddler remains one of the organists at Roscoe and works in a rota with Mrs Joan Edmondson, Mr Jack Anderson and Mrs Kathleen Hall.

Roscoe Church Choir thrived with the help of Mr Allan Herbert and the late Mr Enos Harris. Choir members decided to acquire gowns. Some purchased their own and with the help of a concert, staged by the choir, gowns were bought for all the members. In July 2004 a Service of Blessing was held.

The Choir practises the hymns for the Sunday Services every Friday (organist Joan Edmondson). We perform at various events such as concerts and funerals. At Christmas time we sing carols at a Nursing Home to the residents and their relatives.

Louise Crumbie

ROSCOE STEEL BAND

The Leeds Brotherhood of Steel (hereafter called the Association), was formed in Leeds (date not recorded).

The Objects of the Association were:

1   To provide the benefits and welfare of the inhabitants of West Yorkshire.

2   To establish, secure and maintain a Centre for the better performance of the Association's objectives, to co-operate with any local group, body (eg schools/Education dept), in the Leeds establishment and maintenance of such a centre.

3   To advance education among the inhabitants of the area of benefit, and in particular the task of developing and promoting steel band music as a cultural and artistic heritage, and to teach adults and youths from all cultures to appreciate and play this form of music.

Roscoe Methodist Church was in alliance with this Association, and in January 1984, decided to launch a Steel Band, to orchestral standard. The Revd John Whittle was the minister, and the deaconess was Sister Stella Bullivant. Mrs Gloria Condor, Mr Hugh Condor, Mrs Myrna Tyrell (Girls' Brigade Captain), Mr Allan Herbert (Boys' Brigade Captain) and Mr Arthur France (Co-ordinator), among others, were at the forefront of Roscoe Methodist Church Youth Steel Band.

They requested financial support from various organisations, including Leeds Leisure Services. The estimated cost of the equipment was £5,600.

The group was organised under the guidance of the Steel Band Association, and consisted of youths from Roscoe and also from the community. The tutor was Mr Raymond Joseph, who travelled from Huddersfield. Steel pans were purchased, and rehearsals were three times each week.

The Band made a brilliant start and achieved a fair measure of success in a short time. This was possible because of the initial surge of interest by members of the Boys' and Girls' Brigades, and the regular and disciplined tutoring of Mr Joseph.

The Band played in Roscoe during Morning communion service, and several other occasions. The Band also played at other services in Leeds, including Leeds Town Hall, at the special event of the Girls' Brigade Display.

In the first half of 1985, because of inappropriate behaviour by some members of the Band, and also the difficulty Mr Joseph was experiencing when he tried to travel to Roscoe from his home in Huddersfield, rehearsals were less frequent. There was also a shortage of financial support. Over a period of time the Band folded.

In the 1990s some members of Roscoe including Mr Elbert Moving, Mrs Myrna Tyrell and Miss Sheila Forbes were determined to have a Roscoe Steel Band, and decided to engage another tutor, Mr St Clair Morris. The Paradise Steel Band was St Clair's Band which from 1976 he used to teach the children to play in school. Some of these children attended Roscoe Methodist Church, where on an Easter Sunday the Band played for the Service. Together with the children and some adults in the community, the Band was formed. Over a period of time these players joined another Band and Roscoe Steel Band folded.

Again Sheila Forbes, Steward at Roscoe asked St Clair to get involved, this time with members of the Girls' Brigade. Adult members of the church and the community were also encouraged to learn by St Clair, when he expressed the joys and fulfilment of a Band player. Elbert Moving was the bass player.

The Band played on special Sunday Services, including Easter and Christmas. Eventually, as members of the Band moved out of the area, and Elbert Moving developed pains in his knee, the Band gradually folded again.

(From the Minutes of Roscoe Methodist Church Youth Steel Band and conversations with St Clair Morris, Sheila Forbes and Elbert Moving)

THE WEST INDIAN FAMILY COUNSELLING SERVICE (WIFCOS)

Following the pattern of the early immigrants who were of Irish and Jewish descent, the West Indians also settled in considerable numbers in the inner city of Chapeltown, which is the Chapel Allerton Ward LS7, North East Leeds.

Identifying with the church as a matter of inherited tradition was a priority for most West Indians who emigrated to this country. The then Roscoe Place Methodist Church was accessible within the local community to become the spiritual pinnacle and sustenance, whose Christian expectation had to be met in a strange land.

The first generation West Indians began their emigration to the UK in the early fifties with the exception of those who came much earlier on the SS Empire Windrush especially to be recruited into the military service. During the height of the period of unrestricted immigration, they gravitated to Chapeltown in particular to settle to be near relatives or close friends. The following decades saw rapid growth until the door closed in 1993. In order to make it possible to emigrate, some families made the decision for the husband to take the first plunge to the UK to find work, save money and then send for the wife and children to join the family unit. It was not always feasible for all of the children to travel at the same time. Some had to be left behind with relatives because the hearth had to be cleaned of the ashes as well as maintained during some inconvenient time.

Support Ministry

The Roscoe Place Methodist Church as it was then called was noted for the very warm welcome which the minister and members extended to the West Indians who made contact to engage in worship which they were so much accustomed to in their country of origin. The participation in worship for many who lived mainly in the Leeds 7 & 8 area.

Over a period of years the stresses and strains on West Indian family life in this area of Leeds had revealed themselves in increasing estrangement between spouses, but also, quite specially, in the parent/child relationships which often resulted in teenagers leaving home in increasing numbers.

The staff and leaders of Roscoe Methodist Church had a growing concern for those families, parents and children, both in church life and family situations. Arising out of these concerns, it was our desire that special attention should be given to counselling families experiencing difficult tensions in relationships. We aimed to promote a caring ministry and to foster fellowship; therefore we wished to appoint a Family Counsellor who would specialize in working with West Indian families.

The West Indian Family Counselling Service was started in September 1979 when Mr Emmanuel Kebbe was appointed as a worker/organiser; he who remained in the post until October 1980. After that date the service was temporarily suspended until another worker could be appointed to take up the post from 1st July 1981 when WIFCOS was operative again.

It was intended to offer this service to the whole Caribbean community throughout Leeds, which numbered approximately 25,000, but the worker would be based at Roscoe Methodist Church and would work with the staff and leaders of the church.

The WIFCOS project has a Support and Advisory Committee to whom the worker can turn on a regular basis to share particular difficulties, problems and opportunities. The worker would hopefully have some experience in personal counselling, and have some knowledge and experience of West Indian patterns and culture.

The person appointed would offer support to the leaders of youth groups and organisations in the life of the church, and work with the staff as a member of a team and relate to the community as opportunity arises.

Climate

What an exchange after all? West Indians exchanged the sunshine for the snow, warmth for cold and shoes for boots, to name but a few. Seeing snow for the first time was really a picturesque sight. The climate weatherwise catapulted West Indians into the reliance of their tenacious nature. One had to decide to stay true to their new adventure, or to return to their former destination. Some to a lesser extent would have done just that due to the hostility of the seemingly near arctic conditions that existed in that era.

The climate of work was that of a plentiful nature, which meant that there was an opportunity of choice of jobs available in various industries up and down the country, i.e the motor, textile and engineering industries, to name but a few. The common ground that existed was manual, which based on a basic low pay with over-time hours was made available to the worker. The NHS also provided another source of employment. Other avenues of employment and training were from the NHS direct recruitment.

The New Phase

A new worker, Mrs Mary Saddler, was recruited to resume the vital work with West Indian families through the WIFCOS project. That materialised in June 1981. It could be termed as co-incidental that in the July of the same year, what is known as the riot, or by some preference, the uprising occurred. That was a negative operation which resulted in the arrest of a number of youth who had to be represented in court by the Law Centre solicitors particularly. The community was left in a distraught condition which up to the present time has the scar of some of the shops with shutters still in existence.

The event triggered the Leeds City Council leaders and officers to arrange meetings to engage with youth and others in the community as a fact-finding exercise. It was like a hot potato issue then, but didn't result in any noticeable positive action for the youth of the day.

The new worker was then engaged in some advocacy work with a small number of families whose children had become embroiled in the episode of the riot more by coercion than by will. However, the recording studio which was the burning desire that those young people had put forward to Leeds City Council did not come to fruition in any way. Disillusionment, doom and gloom lasted for decades following. The Mandela Centre came on stream under the umbrella of the then Education Department and the youth workers were trained and employed to work with the young people in the community. The Technorth Project also started in order to empower Afro-Caribbean youngsters who were written off to some degree in the educational system which existed.

Mission and Outreach

The WIFCOS worker was available in the office based at Roscoe from 10am to 1pm to provide a walk-in-service with a strictly confidential code to enable WIFCOS to make progress and stability within the community it was up to serve. There was a variety of problems which were faced by some families, but listening and enabling were the main tools the worker had to use to deal with the issues that were presented.

The term Afro-Caribbean became a definition for the West Indian ethnic group as well as the term Black which could be put down to politics. Racial discrimination was also very prevalent and disconcerting for those who were facing that kind of problem especially in the work place.

In the schools, the issue of racism was deemed to be one of the reasons for the under-achievement which bedevilled the educational progress of black children. That accusation was fiercely shrugged off within the circle of education. However, it is still believed to have had some justification owing to the high level of suspensions that used to be prevalent among black children in some schools.

Networking with some of the other agencies within the community was also necessary to be taken as it proved to be beneficial to the general cause of problem solving.

Roscoe Luncheon Club

The WIFCOS worker found that during the early eighties, the number of sixty plus age group was low among the West Indian community, but at the then Community Centre which existed in Reginald Terrace, LS7, there was a group of West Indian and Polish elders who were meeting to do craft work, socialise and share snacks. In observation, the idea came about to consider the possibility of starting a luncheon club for that age group which would be based at Roscoe under the umbrella of WIFCOS.

Contact regarding this development was made with some local churches to enlist the target group and to encourage their involvement. That resulted in the identification of a volunteer cook who hailed from St Martin's Church and who stayed many years with the lunch club before she took ill. Through social services other volunteers were also found and to complete the team there were also others from Roscoe Church.

158

Roscoe Luncheon Club officially opened in July 1984 and has passed its 25th year. The aim is to enable the older West Indians primarily to acquire a better quality of life by combating isolation and loneliness. There's also the provision of healthy and succulent cultural meals which the members appreciate and enjoy. The worker also is available to give counselling and support to any member who requires that service which remains confidential to individual members.

Other special interests consist of art and craft, gentle exercise done in the chairs and inviting other specialists to come in and share with the group e.g. computer training. They like to go to the Bullring in Birmingham to do some shopping as it is a change of scenery for them. An annual trip to the seaside is usually arranged involving the members in the decision of where they would like to go.

A fully qualified counsellor runs the project with the volunteers who are involved. The Management Committee is responsible to the Church Council.

Transport can sometime cause a worry because the majority of the members have a mobility problem. The ideal situation would be met if there was the slightest chance of acquiring a minibus, but there are no funds available to achieve that status anyhow.

The Luncheon Club meets on Tuesdays and Thursdays weekly. On the whole, the lunch club members are a lively group. The atmosphere is always very lively with the exception of when it's bingo time and no interruption is allowed by anyone who isn't playing the game. There is a time restriction because transport arrangements which require them to leave earlier than in previous times.

Mary Saddler

Roscoe Methodist Church today

APPENDICES

ROLL OF HONOUR
of those connected with this Church
(Roscoe Place Wesleyan Chapel)
who served their Country during the War 1914 – 1919)

A.A.Armstrong
P.J.Armstrong
E.Bennett
G.D.Bottomley
W.W.Armstrong
H.Cooper
F.Darby
A.Dickenson
A.Firth
C.E.Gaunt
W.Gaunt
J.H.Grisdale
F.Harrison
J.H.Hodgson
R.Keighley
P.Marsh
W.L.Matthewman
F.Myers
R.W.Plant
P.Rhodes
W.Richardson
J.Ross
J.R.Simpson
B.Stevenson
J.Stevenson
H.R.Tebb
K.A.P.Thomas
W.F.Vickers
S.C.Ward
F.Wolley

H.Armstrong
W.C.Armstrong
D Bottomley
W.C.Bottomley
H.R.Borrough
F.C.Coleman
W.L.Darby
G.A.Fearnside
C.Garside
L.Gaunt
E.Greenwood
C.Hanson
E.Hawkes
A.W.Jackson
W.Mabane
H.Matthewman
L.Moss
A.Page
N.Reyner
E.Richardson
H.Rippin
B.Simpson
C.E.Smith
F.Stevenson
J.Taroey
J.C.Tessyman
B.R.Vickers
H.Walker
F.Woodroffe

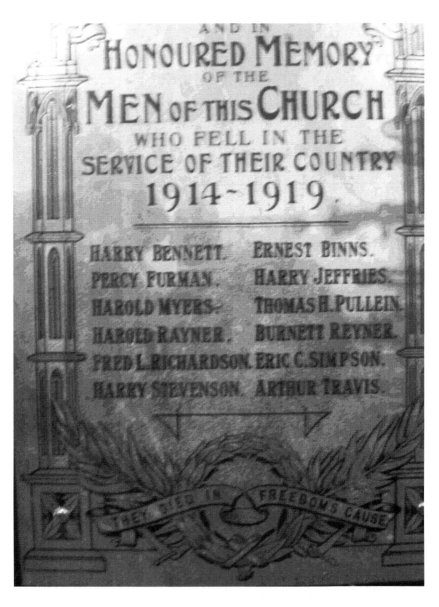

Roll of Honour: men of Roscoe families who died in World War 1

And in
HONOURED MEMORY
of the
MEN OF THIS CHURCH
WHO FELL IN THE
SERVICE OF THEIR COUNTRY
1914 -1919

HARRY BENNETT	ERNEST BINNS
PERCY FURMAN	HARRY JEFFRIES
HAROLD MYERS	THOMAS H. PULLEIN
HAROLD RAYNER	BURNETT REYNER
FRED L. RICHARDSON	ERIC C. SIMPSON
HARRY STEVENSON	ARTHUR TRAVIS

(THEY DIED IN FREEDOM'S CAUSE)

164

New Trustees at this date 14th March 1972
Jessie Peacock
John Connor
Myrna Anita Tyrell
James Arthur Saddler
Sarah Lunn
Lily Atkinson
Ethel Sedman
Charles William Burgess
Charles Eric Griffiths
Allan Joseph Herbert

MINISTERS WHO SERVED
ROSCOE PLACE WESLEYAN CHAPEL
and
ROSCOE METHODIST CHURCH

1862	Rev James Sugden	1929	Rev Wilfred Gower
1867	Rev Josiah Pearson	1934	Rev C Wesley Hickman
1869	Rev John Henshall	1936	Rev H Kenneth Saunders
1870	Rev George E Young	1939	Rev Herbert John Ivens
1871	Rev Stephen P Harvard	1942	Rev J Charlton Blackburn
1872	Rev Henry W Holland	1946	Rev Lewis H Allison
??????		1952	Rev L G Buckingham
1886	Rev William R Stewart	1954	Rev Harry Salmon
1886	Rev William C Kewish	1958	Rev J Russell Moston
1889	Rev F M Parkinson	1962	Rev J Malcolm Furness
1893	Rev W Blackburn Fitzgerald	1965	π Rev D Gerald Bostock
1895	Rev George Norris	1967	π Rev Kenneth Glendinning
1898	Rev Henry Curnow	1968	π Rev Peter B Williamson
1901	Rev Stephen Harper	1970	Rev Michael Chapman
1904	Rev John Elsworth	1972	Rev Trevor S Bates
1907	Rev Walter F Mayer	1972	π Rev Ian G Lucraft
1910	Rev Thomas Rippon	1974	π Rev Raymond Garfoot
1913	Rev John Baker	1981	Rev John Whittle
1915	Rev W R Griffin	1985	Rev Peter A Reasbeck
1919	Rev E Howell Jones	1987	Rev David Whitehall
1921	Rev Frederick W Beaumont	1992	Rev Robert B Creamer
1925	Rev Arthur Phillips	2006	Rev Mark Harwood

NB π indicates a probationer minister

DEACONESSES

1915	Sister Charis ?
1975	Sister Lily Dobbs
1976	Sister Margaret Horn
1982	Sister Stella Bullivant

RESOURCES

We wish to acknowledge the very helpful cooperation of the archivist and staff at **West Yorkshire Archives (Sheepscar) Leeds** for:

1   generous help and advice re the use of **"Tracks in Time"** and the reproduction of portions of Ordnance Survey maps 203.14 and 218.02 of 1910 on page 9 showing Sheepscar and Chapeltown Road, and

2   making available a number of Minute Books etc pertaining to Little London School and Chapel, Roscoe Place Wesleyan Chapel, and Roscoe Place Methodist Church in the 19th and 20th centuries, as follows:

Personal Reminiscences of Roscoe Place Wesleyan Chapel by
   Benjamin Threlfall Vickers written at Willow House April 23rd
   1906
Brunswick Methodist Chapel and Circuit: 1785 – 1966 (WYL 490)
Leeds North East Methodist Circuit 183? - 1996
Roscoe Place Trust minute book (1933 – 1977)
Little London Sunday School Council minute book (1931 – 1935)
   and
   Roscoe Place Sunday School (1952 – 1964)
Roscoe Place Trust minute book 1909 – 1932
Roscoe Place Leader's minute book (1915 – 1945)
Roscoe Place Scrap book containing handbills, notices etc. (1939 –
   1943)
Listing of Joint Trustees at Roscoe Place Special Trustees meeting -
   4th March 1972 – final meeting before Trustees meetings
   abolished by Methodist Church Act 1976 (Ref. WYL 949/162)

Roscoe Methodist Church has made available some of its own
minute books:
Leader's Meeting Minute Book (1963 – 1989)
Church Council Minutes (1974 – 2010)
Finance and Property Committee Minute Book (1975 – 2000)
Pastoral Committee Minute Book (1963 – 1989)

Other:

A Dictionary of Methodism in Britain and Ireland, edited by Dr John Vickers

A History of Modern Leeds, edited by Derek Fraser 1980

The Methodist Conference – Leeds 1956 – Handbook

This Family Business, compiled and published by Benjn. R.Vickers & Sons, Ltd. 1954

Vickers Family reminiscences c/o John Vickers (grandson of BRV)

Spin a Good Yarn, the story of W. Farrar Vickers by Virginia Vickers 1978

John Laycock, Weaver and Organ Builder, by Bryan Hughes

Wesley Guild – The First Hundred Years, by the Revd William Leary 1995

Our thanks go also to:

- **Huddersfield University Archives Department,** West Yorkshire for copy of *Leeds Brunswick Circuit Preachers' Plan of Appointments to Wesleyan Chapels June 4th to September 24th 1871*

- **Yorkshire Post Newspapers** library staff, Leeds for news items and notices re Mr William (Bill) Merritt and Roscoe Place Methodist Church

- **Mr Colin Dews, Leeds Methodist District archivist,** who was an invaluable source of information and support in this venture

- the staff of **peepaltreepress** for their help, support and cooperation in connection with the printing of this book.